W9-BXU-404

GOD IN A BOX

by Frank Callison

GOD IN A BOX

by Frank Callison

A Novel

Faith Publishing Company
Milford, Ohio, U.S.A.

Published by: Faith Publishing Company
                 P.O. Box 237
                 Milford, Ohio 45150-0237
                 United States of America

Additional copies of this book may be acquired by contacting:

For book stores: Faith Publishing Company
                  P.O. Box 237
                  Milford, OH 45150-0237
                  USA
                  Phone: 1-513-576-6400
                  Fax: 1-513-576-0022

For individuals: The Riehle Foundation
                  P.O. Box 7
                  Milford, OH 45150-0007
                  USA
                  Phone: 1-513-576-0032

Copyright © 1996, Frank Callison

ISBN: 1-880033-21-6
Library of Congress Catalog Card No.: 96-083751

All rights reserved. No portion of this book may be transmitted or copied, by any means whatsoever, without the written approval of the publisher.

Scripture references from: *The New American Bible*
                              Saint Joseph Edition
                              Confraternity of Christian
                                 Doctrine;
                              Washington, D.C.; 1970

Front cover illustration: Christian Wilhelmy

Dedication

To my wife Ruth, to me, proof positive of God's goodness.

Chapter 1

". . . to be with you always: the spirit of truth, whom the world cannot accept, since it neither sees him nor recognizes him; but you can recognize him because he remains with you . . ." (*John* 14:16-17).

Tim knew what he was thinking was crazy. "The phone rings the same way each time it rings." There it rang again! "Now tell me that wasn't different," thought Tim. "This is going to be an important call!" This reaction to a common event was strange to Tim. He had learned a long time ago that he could predict nothing. The phone begged for attention for the third time. He thought how foolish he was going to feel when a young lady would say, "Good afternoon, Mr. Sorsen. This is Sally from the Disabled American Veterans calling. Our trucks will be in your neighborhood Friday the . . . ." He grabbed the phone before the answering machine answered. "Hello?" Tim said tentatively—obviously a question rather than a greeting.

His good friend Martin Mills, Vice-President and second in command at Sorsen International Machines, Inc., shouted, "Hey, Tim, you better sit down before I tell you what happened after you left for the board meeting at the bank this morning!"

"I'm sitting down, so tell me."

"Well, you're not going to believe this, but do you remember that sale of fifteen K845 Earth Movers we sold to Israel?"

"Yes, I remember it, and it's about time you stop bragging about it. You've already spent the commission on . . . ."

"Hold on, Tim. They were having trouble with one of the motors and shipped it back for repair or replacement. When we opened the shipping crate in Receiving . . . hang on . . . we found the **Ark**!"

"You found what?"

"You know, the Ark of the Covenant!"

"Martin, this telephone call started off strange. I'm in no mood for jokes! If this is some kind of joke, you can report back to your first job with SIMI, in the mail room!"

"No joke, Tim, we got experts, news men, TV cameras, and cops all over the place! Everybody's asking for you."

"Why me? I don't know anything about it."

"Well, you **are** the president of the company, Tim. Could you come down here right away, please?"

"It'll take me an hour or so to get there."

"How about it if we send the chopper over to pick you up?"

"Is the chopper back from Racine?"

"Yes, the Bell is back, and Carl is waiting for me to give him the nod to pick you up."

"OK. I'll be waiting by the tennis courts. But remember, Martin, if this is some kind of joke—a surprise party or anything like that—nobody involved will hear the last of it!"

"Tim, you have my word on it–this is for real!"

Tim belied his 62 years. He was six feet tall, trim and fit with only a slight paunch. He had a beautiful, well-groomed head of steel-gray, white-frosted hair. Complementing the hair were bushy, brown eyebrows, deep set, blue eyes, and a very tan, clean-shaven face. Tim looked like he should be wearing golf or tennis attire rather than business clothes. The tan was gained, however, from time spent on his sun deck, or at a tanning salon. This was done on weekends so he would not take time away from his business. He only played golf or tennis if he were entertaining business guests.

At the moment he was befuddled as to what to do. This was very unusual for Tim, a person very sure of himself. Did he have time to take a shower? No, of course not. Maybe he would feel better if he had a Scotch and water? No, if this thing is real he would need his wits about him. He went into the kitchen and poured himself a glass of V8. He savored the drink, thinking, "Beats Scotch anytime." Going into the den he pulled out the second volume of the encyclopedia, AN to BA and looked up Ark. It described Noah's Ark. "My God, did Martin mean Noah's Ark? No, no, he said 'the Ark of the Covenant.'" Tim was angry with himself, for he knew how to find data in the encyclopedia. But as he reached for the index to look up the Ark of the Covenant he heard the chopper. He scrambled to the back door while searching his pockets for the house and alarm keys.

The chopper was setting down on the lot next to the tennis courts. What a mess it was making, blowing dust and leaves all over! The big chopper was one of two that SIMI short-term leased to heavy construction contractors. Tim made a dash for the chopper's open door. Once

3

in, he fastened his seat belt and tried to talk to Carl. He knew this was a mistake and quickly put on headphones and mike. "Carl, what the hell is going on at SIMI?"

"I don't know, Mr. Sorsen, and nobody else seems to know! Seems they found something in a motor box we got from Israel."

"Martin said there were a lot of people there!"

"Hey, if you'd tried to drive back, you wouldn't have made it! The streets are jammed with cars and people. You've never seen anything like it!"

"Carl, you say you don't know what they've found?"

"That's right, Sir. They have Shipping and Receiving sealed off."

"Who are 'they,' Carl?"

"I don't know who 'they' are—police, guys with ID tags, and other important looking people. I don't think any of them know what they're doing. They're all running around yelling at each other. Look down there, Mr. Sorsen!"

"My God, Carl, there're thousands of people and cars!"

"That's right, Sir. They came about ten minutes after the news broke on TV and radio."

"Carl, there's a chopper on your pad. You can't set her down."

"I see it, Sir. I'll put it down on the roof over there by Administration."

"Are you sure that's safe, Carl?"

"Sure. I've done it many times, Sir. I'm going in now."

SIMI was very impressive from this aerial view. There were many large and small buildings in a symmetrical pattern. It looked like a large manufacturing company rather than a distributor of heavy construction machines. The reason for SIMI's vast size was that some of the special machines were assembled here.

Martin was way ahead of them and was waiting on the roof as Carl set down, even though they had made no radio contact. Tim was out of the chopper and running toward Martin when the chopper was still inches off the roof.

Martin Mills at fifty was what the ladies call a "Hunk." He played college football at CU and tried out for the Kansas City Chiefs. He was six feet two, two hundred twenty-five pounds, with long, over-the-collar, dark brown hair. His handsome face usually wore a smile—a real smile that went with his hands on approach to people. He was a toucher; often he would put his arm around a person's shoulders or pat their shoulder when talking to them. As a salesman, he was almost impossible to resist.

Martin put his hand on Tim's shoulder and said, "Come inside and put this on."

"What the hell is this?"

"It's your ID tag. It'll let people know who you are."

"Damn it, Martin, this is my company. I own fifty-one percent of the stock, and I don't need any ID card!"

"Put it on, Tim. There are a lot of people here who don't know you."

"I'm going to my office. You get everybody and anybody from the company who can tell me what's going on, so I can appraise the situation."

"I'm not sure if I can find anybody in all of this mess, but I'll do my best. I'm sure there are other people who want to talk to you, Tim."

"I'll talk to others when I know and understand what's going on!"

Since Tim had landed on the roof next to Administration, he did not have far to go to his office. There was a uniformed police officer by his office door. "I'm sorry, Sir, you can't go in here."

"The hell I can't! This is my office, and I'm going in! May I see some kind of legal document that says I can't go into my own office?!"

The nervous young officer, obviously fresh out of the police academy, squeaked his reply, "May I see your ID, Sir? Yes, Sir, I see that this is your office, but my instructions are that no one can enter here, Sir! If you'll wait here, Sir, I'll check and see if it's OK for you to enter."

When the officer walked away, Tim opened the door and walked in. This door was Tim's private entrance, one of two. The other entrance was from a reception office, his secretary's office. The office was spacious with two heavy wooden entrance doors and a third door to a private lavatory. It had long windows overlooking the grounds of SIMI. The room was finished with dark wood paneling, furnished with leather chairs and couch, and three large oil paintings of outdoor scenes—lake, forest, and mountains. The office would remind those who have been there of Tim's home, designed by the same interior decorator.

He sat down at his very clean desk, punched his secretary on the keypad. No response! He looked at the desk clock–4:23. "She must have left already," he thought. "No, June would not have left with all this going on. She must be somewhere on the grounds."

Martin, Jim Nelson, and Guy Rivers came into his office unannounced, which surprised Tim until he remembered that June was not at her desk.

Martin said, "These are all I could find, Tim. There's so much going on out there, I can't find anybody else. Nobody will answer their page. Let us tell you what we know, starting with Guy here."

Just then three uniformed police officers entered the office. The one in the center had a chest full of ribbons and "scrambled egg" on his hat.

Tim shouted at them, "Gentlemen, please wait in the outer office. We have a meeting going on here!"

Ribbons-at-attention replied in a deep, very relaxed radio announcer's voice, "We are very sorry for this intrusion, Sir. This is an emergency situation, and we cannot wait to observe formalities. Officer Lofquist informs me that you are Timothy R. Sorsen, president of this company."

"I am, and I ask you by what authority you are here? Has this company been involved in any wrong doing? Show me a legal document that allows you to take over my company and my buildings!"

In an even more relaxed voice, as compared to Tim's excited voice, the decorated officer replied, "I have no such legal document, Mr. Sorsen, and we'll gladly leave if you'll tell me how you would protect yourselves from the thousands of people who are out there trying to get in and would certainly trample these premises. Even if we stay, we may not be strong enough to stop them! We have asked the Governor for his help with the National Guard!"

Tim thought about the scene he had witnessed from the chopper earlier and decided he'd better do some listening instead of talking.

In a voice an octave lower, Tim said, "I'm sorry. Won't you please come in? I'm very disturbed because I have no idea what is going on here, and that's the purpose of this meeting."

"Sounds like a great idea, Mr. Sorsen. We would like to join you because we, too, would like to know how and why all this started. By the way, I'm Chief Lyle Johnson. This is Officer Lofquist and Officer Cramer."

Tim, feeling he was still in the driver's seat, continued, "Jim, please find everybody chairs. Martin, where were we?"

"We were going to start with Guy, since he discovered the Ark or whatever it is."

"Well, I didn't really discover it, Martin. Walters in Receiving opened the motor box and came over to me and said, 'You better come over here an' have a look, that ain't no motor in that there crate.' I looked, and just as Walters said, that wasn't a motor in that box! You know the rest."

"No, I don't! What was in the box?"

"Well, at first we couldn't tell much. It looked like two statues of lions with wings and human heads. So we could see better, Walters and I disassembled the motor box. We didn't want to lift it out of the box for fear of damaging it. We were right. It was two statues of lions with spread wings and human heads. They sat on a base about four feet by two by two feet. It was all gray in color, but we noticed that the gray was dust and dirt. So we wiped some off with a shop rag, and it was a blackish color. Right away Walters said it was gold. I said, 'Sure, Walters. Black Gold.' He said, 'No, it is gold. I can see it where I scraped off some of the crusted dirt.' He said, 'I'll be right back. We've got some ammonia here some-where. It makes a pretty good jewelry cleaner.' Anyway Walters got the ammonia and a couple more shop rags. It didn't take him long until he had a gold shiny spot on one of the statues. We did another spot on the base with the same results. The whole blooming thing is gold or gold-plated! We didn't know what to do so we covered it with a tarp so no one could see it. Then we went to get Mr. Mills, and he knows the rest."

"Tim, I was as flabbergasted as Guy and Walters. After they showed it to me, we covered it back up. There were only six people working in Receiving right then so we sent them over to Shipping to do some busy work."

"Why so secretive, Martin. What did you think you had?"

"Hey, Tim, you had to be there. You've got to see this thing to appreciate how we felt opening this crate, expecting a diesel engine to be in it, and finding maybe a priceless heirloom. OK, let me go on. Not knowing where to start, I went to the sales office and pulled the files on sales to Israel. With a little help from Riley and Doris, we found a file on a problem with the engine of one of the K845s. After a lot of correspondence, we suggested that they ship the engine back to us for either repair or replacement, probably the latter. There was absolutely nothing about them shipping us anything else. If it was a machinery part sent to us by mistake, I could see how that could happen, but not this.

"We didn't call Israel because of the time difference. I called Carl Livingston over at the Museum of Natural History to come over. You remember Carl, Tim. You met him at my place at Cora's wedding."

"No, I don't remember, Martin, but please go on."

"Well, I called Carl and described the heirloom, artifact, whatever it is, to him. Right away he says, 'My God, I'll be right over,' and hung up. I don't know how, but he was here in twenty minutes, all excited and wide-eyed! We showed Carl our would-be motor, and he was beside himself. He wanted to use a phone. I told him I thought we ought to keep this to ourselves until we know what we have here. He said, 'Man do you know what you have here, or what I think you have? Martin, I think this is the Ark of the Covenant! Now, I'll need the help of my colleagues to determine if it is, in fact, the Ark.' I asked him if they could be trusted, and he said, 'Of course.' He went into Guy's office and made some calls. After that all hell broke loose. He not only called his colleagues, he also called the media! All you have to do is walk around SIMI to see what's happened since then!"

"That's the very first thing I want to do, Martin, starting with that piece of art we received from Israel."

"Mr. Sorsen, if you don't mind, Officers Lofquist, Cramer, and I will have to tend to other matters at this time. We thank everyone for the information about this mysterious shipment. If you need me, just ask any police officer to contact me."

"Thank you, Chief Johnson, and thank you for your patience with me."

The Chief nodded.

Because Shipping and Receiving was clear across SIMI, Martin looked for a couple of golf carts used by the engineering department and other staff members to get around the grounds. He could only find one, so they all squeezed in.

Most of SIMI's buildings were elongated, one-story, red brick buildings, with windowed sides. The administration building, from where they had come, was three stories and squarish. The rest of the buildings were large elongated metal buildings, like towering aircraft hangers. The grounds around the buildings were landscaped with grass and shrubs, except three big parking areas where huge yellow earth movers, graders, and other construction machines were orderly parked. They took one of the clearly marked blacktop roads to S&R.

There were at least one hundred people milling around outside of Receiving. A big share of them had cameras or camcorders. Chet Ryan, SIMI's head of security and a retired Lieutenant Colonel from the military police, waved to them as they approached. Chet, who was made up of a mixture of leather and regulations, said, "Sorry about the mess here, Sir. Things have gotten out of hand. I couldn't keep these people out. Most of them came in with the police and sheriff's department. We're watching the media and the police alike for any improprieties, Sir."

"Do the best you can, Chet. I understand your problem. We would like to go into Receiving. Where would you like us to park the cart?"

"I'll see that it gets parked, Sir. But I'm not sure that they'll let you into Receiving; they are not admitting anyone to the building."

"Thank you, Chet. We'll give it a try."

They found the large bay doors, which are normally open, closed. They went to the Receiving office door but were stopped by a uniformed police officer who said, "Sorry, gentlemen, you cannot go in this building."

Pointing to his ID, Tim said, "I'm Tim Sorsen, President of this company. This is my building."

After looking at his note pad, the officer said, "Sorry, Sir, you are not on the approved list of those who can enter."

"Chief Johnson said if I were to have any problems I should ask a police officer to contact him. Would you contact the chief, please!"

The officer hesitated a moment, then took his radio from his belt and spoke into it, "300, 378." After a short time his radio spoke back, "378, 300." The officer again spoke into the radio, "Sir, I have a...*break*.... May I see your ID, Sir? Sir, I have a Tim Sorsen who would like admittance to SIMI's Receiving Department, and he suggested I contact you."

"378, that is **Mr.** Tim Sorsen. Most certainly let Mr. Sorsen and his party in any building he wishes to enter. This is his company, and we're here only to protect him and his company. Is 324 with you?"

"No, Sir. He's inside Receiving."

"Have Mr. Sorsen and his party wait there, and I'll have Romero come out for him."

"Copy, Sir, 378."

"378, 300, clear."

As the officer was returning his radio to his belt it said, "324, 300, respond channel B." Tim was very aware that all of this was strictly PR for his benefit by the chief. The officer said, "The chief says…."

Tim waved him off saying, "I copied, too. We'll wait for Romero."

In a short time the door opened and Romero, an officer of obviously higher rank, came out, hand extended, saying, "Mr. Sorsen?"

Tim took the extended hand replying, "I'm Sorsen."

"Please excuse all this precaution, Sir. I just talked to the chief, and he would like me to assist you in any way I can."

"Thank you. I would just like to get into my building here!"

Like a very gallant doorman, Romero stepped aside and waved them in.

SIMI's Receiving was one of the metal buildings, a large airplane hanger type building with smaller bay doors than a hanger. It was very bright inside with good lighting plus sky lights. Tim hadn't walked very far when he stopped and thought, "**Oh no**, there's that feeling again that I had earlier when I received Martin's phone call!" Tim then said aloud, "There's something in here!"

They all looked at Tim, waiting for him to define, when Guy interjected, "They just painted the floor over there in the northeast corner." That was not what Tim meant, but he started walking, following Martin. They stopped and spread out to view the shipment from Israel.

Tim could not get his breath and started gasping for air, and coughing.

Martin said, "What's wrong, Tim?"

Tim finally got control of his breathing and said, "I don't know. It must be that paint!"

The statuary was gray except for three bright gold spots with blackish borders on it. The statues were indeed as Guy had described them—two lions with spread wings and human heads. The two almost identical creatures were facing each other, mounted on a base that had two poles through two rings on each side. The poles looked like they were meant to lift or to carry the statuary.

Tim stared at the piece of art. He had the feeling that he wanted to see more. He had excellent vision, but kept blinking his eyes, trying to see better.

Coming back to reality, Tim asked the people around the statuary, "Where is Carl Livingston?"

"I'm Carl Livingston."

"I'm Tim Sorsen. They tell me you think that this art is the Ark of the Covenant?"

"We're not certain, Tim. But if this is a fake, it's a mighty good one."

"How soon will you know if this is the real Ark?"

"Weeks, maybe months."

"I understand that you called the media and are responsible for this chaos."

"I did, Sir, for this is a breakthrough that the world's been waiting for! It's a very important find, substantiating world and biblical history. If it's not important, then why are thousands of people out there in the streets, and why is there, as you say, 'chaos' here? If you'll excuse me, Sir, I have to get back to my examination."

"You'd better examine your assets, Livingston, because I'll have you in court over this!"

June, a very attractive redhead with an exciting, unadorned face, touched Tim's shoulder. "I'm so glad you're here, Mr. Sorsen. Isn't this just terrible? I've tried to reach you everywhere. Each time I called they said you'd just left!"

"Thank you for your efforts, June. Is there anything I should know?"

"You probably know more about this by now than I do, but right now the Governor is waiting to see you in your office."

"Lloyd is here?"

"Yes, Sir, in your office."

"Lloyd, it's good to see you! How's the golf game coming; have you broken 100 yet?"

Lloyd looked like a governor. He was Tim's age, with coal black hair, except at the roots, a black mustache, black suit, and a campaign smile.

"My golf game is as good as yours any day, Sorsen. It's good to see you, Tim! Sorry I took your parking place."

"Oh, was that your chopper on the north pad?"

"Not mine, it belongs to the state."

"Does that mean you're here on state business?"

"Just trying to find out what's going on here, Tim."

"Well, as everybody seems to be telling each other around here, you probably know as much as I do by now, Lloyd. We received this thing from Israel—what a few would-be archaeologists, scientists, and expert experts say could be the Ark of the Covenant. It came in a motor box that was supposed to have a motor—a diesel engine—in it to be repaired or replaced."

"How many witnessed the opening of the box?"

"Just one, a man named Walters. I don't know his first name. He opened the motor box."

"Could this be something that this man Walters created? Maybe he belongs to a cult or far-out religion, trying to establish his religion."

"The only cult Walters belongs to is at Logan's Bar and Grill. Walters can't even create a clean Receiving Department. Besides he would have to have brought the thing in, in his lunch box."

"Do you have any idea of where this 'thing,' as you call it, might have come from?"

"Hey, I thought it came from Israel. I didn't think about it coming from anyplace else. To clear this up, I'll just give Israel a call and find out what they sent and why!"

"No, I think a better approach would be to wait and see if they contact you with an explanation."

"I'm afraid, because of business ethics, we're stuck with acknowledging receipt of the shipment."

"In the meantime you're stuck with a crowd of people on the outside and inside of your business. Chief Johnson contacted me as soon as the story broke. I think the situation is in good hands with Johnson."

"Governor, did you see the people and the cars out there? By tomorrow it'll be much worse!"

"I saw them the same as you, Tim. As a governor, I've studied mass frenzy and mass hysteria. Each one has a peak. I think this has or will peak early. While the media created this chaos, it will unknowingly defuse the excitement. Already the networks are interviewing their experts, archaeologists, scientists, and historians who are skeptical of anything they didn't discover or find for themselves.

"The networks are repeating that there's no need to come to this site when their best seat would be in front of their television or radio. We have promised to share the latest current news with all the networks in return for their cooperation."

"I don't know, Lloyd. There are an awful lot of people out there!"

"I know, Tim, but don't underestimate Johnson and his men and women and the size of his force. Let's just relax a bit and try to solve some of this mystery. For instance. . . ."

Via electronics, June interrupted them saying, "Excuse me, Sir, for this interruption, but I have something of importance about the shipment from Israel. May I bring it in?"

"Yes, of course, June."

"Mr. Sorsen, I just received this fax addressed to you and Mr. Mills."

Tim slowly read the fax.

"Look at this, Lloyd. This solves the problem of where the thing came from! This is a fax from the Israeli government, stating that they shipped an artifact to us by mistake in place of a defective motor. They would like us to ship it back as per instructions which will be given to us by a team on the way from Israel—for security reasons—to help us prepare it for shipping. We're to confirm by fax. They say they've been unable to reach us by telephone."

"Well, that solves one of your problems, Tim."

"Hey, Lloyd, that solves all of my problems. All I have to do now is ship that thing back and get back to running a business!"

"I'm not so sure it's going to be all that simple, Tim. Your memory is very short. Have you looked out of the window in the last few minutes? Do you want to be the one who tells them you're shipping the Ark back to Israel? I'm not sure how our bureaucratic government is going to react to all of this either. They may step in and muddy up the waters."

"Lloyd, this—whatever it is—obviously belongs to Israel!"

"Believe me, Tim, this ain't over till the plump lady says it is. Let's call it a night. It's 10:36!"

"My God, is it that late?" Tim electronically put his thumb on June's ear saying, "June, are you out there?"

"Yes, Mr. Sorsen, how may I help you?"

"You can help me by going home. Thanks for staying so late, June. We'll tackle this again in the morning."

"Good night, Mr. Sorsen."

"Tim, can I give you a lift home? I mean that literally. Because you came in a helicopter, you must have left your car at home. Since I came in a helicopter, too, it seems to be the only answer."

Tim was sorry about his helicopter ride home because it only excited the news people in front of his house even more than they were! He had a difficult time gaining entrance to his home through the questions he had answers for, but being "world wise," did not answer. They were still out there. Tim could hear them. He tried to turn the ringer off the phone, but evidently Wally, Tim's house-keeper, a disabled Indian guide he befriended on several hunting trips to Canada, had already turned them off.

The Sorsen estate was a fifteen-room house on three beautiful landscaped acres. It was enclosed behind stone pillars and a wrought iron fence. It had all the amenities such as tennis courts, enclosed pool, and putting green. The interior was very masculine with beamed ceilings, heavy wood and leather furniture, and bare hardwood floors. The home did not necessarily reflect Tim's per-sonality, as it was the design of the interior decorator.

Tim poured himself a Scotch and water, sat down in his recliner, and adjusted it as if the Scotch and the chair

17

would end the dream and bring him peace. It didn't work. He kept this strange feeling that he did not understand. He knew with confidence that he had a quick and very capable mind to cope with life and its roadblocks and surprises. Tim also felt he was a religious man. Well, he went to church regularly, supported the Church, was active in the Men's Club. Throughout this he did not want to think about what this would mean to the world if this were the real Ark of the Covenant! "My God," he thought, "Did I really see the Ark of the Covenant?" Tim realized he was covered with goose bumps and there were tears in his eyes!

Jumping up, Tim went to pour himself another Scotch and water, and then, thinking better of it, went to the kitchen and poured a juice glass of V8 and went off to get ready for bed, never returning for the orphaned V8.

Chapter 2

"Then the cloud covered the meeting tent, and the glory of the LORD filled the Dwelling" (*Exodus* 40:34).

Wally was in the kitchen fixing breakfast. The kitchen was large. It had a quaint charm and a little bit of clutter which the rest of the house lacked. There was an oak table with six chairs where Tim and Wally ate most of their meals, unless they had guests. A four-shelf bookcase along the wall beside the table was filled with cookbooks. There were pots, pans, and other utensils hanging over a work table and over the stainless steel and cast-iron gas stove. Two of the walls were lined with cupboards, with counter space the length of both.

Wally was almost six feet tall. If you asked him, he would say that he was six feet. Viewed from the side, Wally looked very thin and slight. A frontal view, however, gave him the appearance of a larger man, for he had broad shoulders and narrow hips. He had medium brown skin, coal black eyes, and shiny black hair pulled back into a short pony tail. He most always wore brown jeans with a loud Indian-print sport shirt, moccasins or western boots. Wally carried his right arm across his mid-section, parallel with his belt. His arm had been injured in a hunting accident when he was a youth. He was unable to straighten the arm out and had to carry it in that position. The arm was movable at the shoulder, and he could perform most tasks like driving and his household chores with ease. "You're up early," said Wally.

"I have some problems at SIMI, Wally."

"So I see, Sir, by the TV."

"Would you get the Mercedes out, while I finish dressing?"

"Yes, Sir. Would you like me to drive?"

"No, Wally. You stick around here and try and keep the media from breaking in. Better keep your phones off, too."

The traffic and crowds around SIMI were much better, but there were many police and police cars visible. The waiting room to his office had four men standing around June's desk. Tim immediately recognized one of them as Secretary of State, William Bates. The Secretary looked like your friendly, round, bald bartender who was uncomfortable in a business suit.

"Mr. Sorsen, Secretary Bates and these other gentlemen are here to see you."

"Good morning, Bill. Do I call you 'Mr. Secretary'?"

"How are you, Tim? What do old friends usually call each other?"

"I'm fine, Bill. What are you doing at SIMI? Did you bring me a contract for a hundred earth movers?"

"No, Tim. I'm here about that unidentified shipment you received."

"I thought it had been identified, Bill. Isn't it the Ark?"

"That's not yet been ascertained. We're going to have to do a lot more research and examinations to find out what it is and where it came from."

"It came to us from Israel."

"I'm afraid that's not the case, Tim. Did you check the shipping case and the bill of lading?"

"No, but I assumed we did when we received it."

"It was never received. Your people were in the process of receiving it when they discovered it was not what they thought it was. True, the bill of lading does specify the contents to be a defective diesel engine, but it was shipped from Canada."

"Tim, may we go into your office to discuss this after I introduce you to these gentlemen?"

Tim nodded, looking at the others with apprehension.

"This is Fred Sevent of the State Department, Walter Friends of the FBI, and Frank Speer of the Secret Service."

Tim shook hands with the men saying, "What have I done to deserve this?" Bill smiled. The others' faces would, like the shipment, have to be examined to see if they were smiling.

Tim led the way into his office saying, "Please hold my calls, June."

When inside and seated, Secretary Bates said, "Could you call Mr. Mills in, please?"

Tim lifted the phone and pressed one number and said, "Mary Lou, is Martin in?" After a pause, "Good morning, Martin. Could you come into my office, please?" After another pause, "Yes, Martin, it is very important."

"Now, Bill, what is this about the shipment coming from Canada?"

Martin came through the side door to Tim's office.

"Martin, I would like you to mee...."

"I have already met everyone, Tim."

"Bill tells me our shipment came to us from Canada."

"That's right, Tim. We just discovered this about a half

hour ago. It was the Secret Service who brought it to our attention that the bill of lading shows the shipment coming from SENCO Ltd. in Ontario, Canada. Also, SENCO has called twice this morning asking us to return the shipment."

"Then how did Israel get into all of this?"

"We assumed it was from Israel because this shipment came in the motor box we sent to Israel to return the defective engine. The motor box—a shipping crate actually—had the engine's description and serial number stenciled on it."

"I'm confused, Martin."

"Join the club, Tim. We're checking with Red Ball to find out dates, times, and from where the shipment actually originated."

Bates added a few more ingredients to this strange recipe for intrigue, "Tim, my office has been contacted by both the Israeli and Canadian governments, asking for its return. In each case we asked for a detailed description of the shipment. Both described the shipping container in detail, but could not, or would not, describe the contents."

"Until we have some kind of valid proof of ownership, we are not shipping it anywhere!"

June's unignorable, pleasant voice interrupted, "Mr. Secretary, the gentlemen you expected have arrived."

"Tim, do you have a larger place where we could continue this?"

"Yes, we can go to the conference room. June, will you have the gentlemen go to the conference room, please."

"Yes, Mr. Sorsen."

The conference room, like all the executive offices, was paneled with dark wood. A large dark oak table was surrounded by twelve leather swivel chairs. The room had three large windows with overhead defused lighting.

Six entered the conference room by one door and four by another. There was some confusion. Bates said, "Gentlemen, please take a seat anywhere, and I'll introduce everyone. Better still, let's go around the table and let everybody introduce themselves with name and title. I'll start. I'm William Bates, Secretary of State."

"Tim Sorsen, President of SIMI."

"Martin Mills, Vice President of SIMI."

"Fred Sevent, State Department."

"Walter Friends, FBI Agent."

"Frank Speer, Secret Service Agent."

"Rabbi Greenberg. I work for God." All smiled or chuckled in relief.

"Father Conely, Communication Director, Archdiocese of Chicago."

"Arthur Chase, Baptist Minister."

"Bishop John Cilse, Methodist Council. I might add that we are here to represent the Council of Churches for all denominations."

Secretary Bates quickly got back in the driver's seat saying, "We have invited these representatives of the Council of Churches here today to make sure we in no way offend any religion or desecrate the alleged Ark. Today we are going to open up the Ark and see what is inside, with the supervision of these gentlemen."

Tim asked, "I know there is a description in the Bible of the Ark, but it escapes me. Does what we have seem to fit that description?"

Bishop Cilse started to open his Bible, when Rabbi Greenberg said in a loud, low, and very clear voice, "A very popular Christian version has it: '*You shall make an Ark of acacia wood, two and a half cubits long, one and a half cubits wide, and one and a half cubits high. Plate it inside and out with pure gold, and put a molding of gold around the top of it. Cast four gold rings and fasten them on the four supports of the Ark, two on one side and two on the opposite side.*

"'Then make poles of acacia wood and plate them with gold. These poles you are to put through the rings on the side of the Ark, for carrying it; they must remain in the rings of the Ark and never be withdrawn. In the Ark you are to put the commandments which I will give you.'"

Rabbi Greenberg hesitated, looking at Father Conely who was following in his Bible. Father Conely continued: *"'You shall then make a propitiatory of pure gold, two cubits and a half long, and one and a half cubits wide. Make two cherubim of beaten gold for the ends of the propitiatory, fastening them so that one cherubim springs direct from each end. The cherubim shall have their wings spread out above, covering the propitiatory with them. This propitiatory you shall then place on top of the Ark.'"*

"What the heck is a cubit?"

"A cubit, Mr. Sorsen," said Bishop Cilse, "is from the tip of your index finger to the tip of your elbow. When the Ark was built, they had no other way of measuring. This length, of course, varied from one man to another. For the average man it is about eighteen inches."

"How's that match up with our Ark?"

Martin answered, "Carl Livingston gave us measurements of . . . let's see, he converted it from metric for me. Yes, here it is, 3 feet 8 and 5/64 inches by 2 feet 2 and 15/16 inches by 2 feet 2 and 5/8 inches."

Bates challenged the knowledge of these men, "Gentlemen, any guesses as to what will be in the Ark?" No one replied.

"Rabbi Greenberg, what will we find in the Ark?"

"Nothing."

"Father Conely?"

"I agree, nothing."

"Bishop Cilse?"

"It will be empty."

"Reverend Chase?"

"It should be empty. A very popular belief is that, if the Ark were found, it would contain the tablets of stone, etched with ten commandments. The Ark might have contained these at one time, but they were replaced by the Laws of the Covenant. Later these scrolls were transferred to the sanctuary in the temple."

"It sounds as if the Ark had lost some of its importance?"

"It did. The Ark just slowly disappears in the Bible."

Tim opened his mouth to speak and June's voice came out saying, "Mr. Sorsen, advise Mr. Bates that it is twenty minutes to nine."

"Thank her for me, Tim."

"Thanks, June."

"The reason your secretary reminded me of the time is that the opening, if you will, is at 9:00 a.m., so I suggest we go over to the Receiving building, gentlemen."

Receiving was a mass of electric cords, lights, TV cameras, camera cameras, people, and the ugly shouting sounds they make when they are excited and impatient with each other. Tim recognized John Frost of NBC and Alan Larson of ABC. "They sure got here in a hurry," he thought.

There were about thirty folding chairs in front of the mis-sent shipment. Bates led his entourage to the very front seats. The seats behind them very quickly filled. There was a lot of small talk such as, what the value of the Ark would be, how old it was, and that it probably was a phony. Someone suggested it was a publicity stunt by SIMI.

There was no formal program; it would have been better to watch it on TV to know what was going on. The great orators of the TV news were describing what was going on and what was about to happen, all in detail.

Tim was in earshot of one network commentator who was saying, "What we are about to see is simply a performance of duty by Receiving Department employees of SIMI. When a shipment is received, if packaged, it is opened and its contents examined for damage, counted for number, matched to a purchase order or to a work order. In other words, they determine where the shipment goes from here.

"What makes this news is that the inner container of this shipment could be a priceless artifact of the ancient world. Some contend this would be further proof of ancient Scripture, the Bible.

"The opening of this alleged Ark is strongly opposed, and I emphasize strongly opposed, by both the Israeli and Canadian governments. Both contend that the shipment was sent by them, by mistake, and they ask for its immediate return.

"Let us now direct your attention to the two men approaching the Ark. The gentleman in the blue shirt and tie is Mr. Guy Rivers, a fifteen-year employee and manager of SIMI's Receiving Department. The gentleman in the plaid shirt and blue jeans is Mr. Wiley Walters, a twenty-eight year employee of SIMI. These men are about to lift the propitiatory that we described earlier." He paused, waiting for the propitiatory removal. He never resumed talking!

Guy and Walters removed the propitiatory. Guy's face contorted and tears immediately welled in his eyes as he looked into the Ark. Walter's face lighted with the glee of a child receiving a new puppy for Christmas!

All sound stopped, yet the sound was beautiful. TV cameras that were supposed to pan the Ark and the audience froze. One network's camera froze on a door, another on the floor full of electrical cords. CNN's camera froze on one side of the Ark. There was a pleasant smell, yet there was no smell. Tim sat, looked, and cried. Receiving was very beautiful, even though it was painted in five faded colors with harsh lighting. There was laughter of glee mixed with happy sobbing which was enhanced when they echoed back from the drab metal building. This lasted for an eternity of six minutes, which must have panicked the network's hordes of VPs watching! Guy, robot-like, stooped to pick up the propitiatory, motioning to Walters who followed Guy's lead, and they placed the propitiatory back on the Ark. Those moments of real peace that Tim—and seemingly the rest—experienced, a span where they saw, smelled, tasted, touched, and heard a moment where there was no tomorrow and no yesterday, disappeared when the Ark was closed.

Secretary Bates stood up, and looking at Guy asked, "Why did you close the Ark?"

"Because it was empty! We will mark on our receiving report that the Ark—excuse me, the inner container—was empty. The shipment will be listed as a golden chest, four pieces in all, weighing 312 pounds."

Bates with raised voice replied, "But no one else had a chance to see inside!"

"Sir, the cover was off for seven or eight minutes, and there was nothing to see."

Someone in the back shouted, "It was six minutes and ten seconds."

Speaking to the media, Bates asked, "Did you people get all the pictures and views you wanted?"

There was a series of angry and disappointed "No"s.

There were also mumbling-like sounds, for there was wonderment and confusion among the media as to why they, who were among the very best, failed to get even one picture or view on camera of the interior of the Ark. Why there were six minutes of silence on radio and TV with no description of the Ark's interior or its contents! The only view the outside world got was CNN's side view of the Ark with Guy and Walters removing and replacing the propitiatory!

The din got worse as technicians talked to cameramen, program directors yelled at technicians, and cameramen and reporters talked to themselves. And TV and radio commentators were trying to explain to the world what happened, when they did not know what happened!

Secretary Bates tried to get everyone's attention without success. Walter Friends of the FBI stood up and folded his folding chair and banged it on a metal support post of the building, getting Bates the attention he needed. "Gentlemen, let's regroup and see what we can do to rectify the situation. This was totally unrehearsed, so there is no blame here.

"As you know we are here today through the hospitality of SIMI." He paused as if he expected some recognition. He got none. Continuing, "The item of all our attention is a shipment of rare artwork received by SIMI from a yet to be ascertained source. What you have witnessed was SIMI's normal receiving procedure. We have with us Mr. Tim Sorsen, President of SIMI. I'm sure if we ask Mr. Sorsen if we could repeat the examination of the shipment for you of the media, and for the viewing of the general public, he would oblige us."

General response was, "Yea, let's do it!"

Tim said nothing, only motioned to Guy who took hold of two corners of the chest's cover, waiting for Walters to do the same. There were sounds of scrambling, for many were not prepared for the suddenness of Guy and Walters. This time, faces showed concern, even fear, as if they were not sure they wanted the reopening they asked for! The silence again was uncommon, followed by the commentators' voices.

Tim could overhear the same commentator he heard before describing the two SIMI's employees removal of the top of the coffer. All networks, as if they were one, focused on the interior of the artifact. It came as little surprise that the Ark was empty after Guy had stated that it was empty. The cameras played on the inside of the chest. Some with scientific minds noted that the inside of the Ark was not encrusted. It sparkled and glittered from the lights and flashes used by TV and news photographers. Tim's commentator questioned why the interior was not gray like the rest of the Ark.

After some viewing, and when the commentators ran out of descriptive words, some thought of the first opening. They felt they owed their audiences some explanation of what had happened. They looked around for experts to interview, but there were none. They tried from their own limited knowledge of such a phenomenon, which was none, and only confused the viewers more.

Tim sat with elbows on his knees, head bowed, staring at his feet, thinking to himself about this happening, "My God, maybe the box wasn't empty!" He was feeling very depressed, a sadness he had never felt before! He felt he had found something he had been searching for all of his life and lost it in the blinking of an eye! He then thought, "That's strange. I thought I had everything I ever wanted. Now, I desperately want 'that,' but I don't know what 'that' is!"

The rest of Tim's day was as hectic as the first. If he had been asked to recall the happenings, he would probably only remember about ten percent. However, it did seem to quiet some. The police had some success in dispersing the crowds, and there were fewer media at the front gate. Also relieving was the fact that Secretary Bates and the other government agencies took over his problems. They would find out who shipped It, who owned It, and directly deal with the parties involved with It. In the meantime It was to be considered the sole property of SIMI!

At 6:30 p.m., before leaving for the day, Tim felt compelled to see the Ark one more time. He went to Receiving and was admitted by the police guard. He wandered around the Ark. In all the excitement of the day he had only one view of one side. It was simply beautiful, obviously handmade. It did not have the modern look of precision. He could imagine how spectacular it would be if the dirt were removed and it had been cleaned and polished!

He looked for a chair, but all of the folding chairs had been removed. He found a crate containing a large sump pump close to the Ark. He started to sit down, changed his mind and took a step toward the Ark, thinking, "I would like to touch it." He stood there for a moment and then retreated to the crate and sat down. "You are afraid of the Ark, aren't you? Well, maybe it's not right, I don't know," thought Tim.

Tim really wanted to relax with the Ark and collect himself, to analyze what had taken place. This was a new experience for the sixty-two year old who had always been able to be abreast of or steps ahead in understanding any situation. He continued looking at the Ark, thinking about his thoughts this morning when he wondered, "Maybe the Ark was not empty the first time it was opened. What could have been in it that would have such a profound effect on those present? Was it some strange gas, a ghost, or spirit?"

Tim laughed to himself about it being a ghost or spirit. He continued to sit staring at the Ark. He began to become very uncomfortable, thinking, "If there were something in the Ark this morning it could still be in the building!" He started looking around the building. He looked up through the metal beams and said aloud, "I would like to talk to you."

Although there was no sound, the answer was, *"What would you like to talk about, my son?"* A prickly feeling started at Tim's spine and went up his neck! He jumped to his feet and started the long walk to the door. He walked slowly at first, picking up speed as he went. He tried whistling as if he was not full of fear. He reached the door, stepped through, and was greeted by a loud **"Freeze"** and a policeman with a drawn gun!

"Oh, I'm sorry! I just came on duty and wasn't told that there was someone in the building." Tim, who could not speak, gave him half a smile and the wave of a hand and walked to the golf cart.

He went straight to his carport, getting into his Mercedes and headed for home. Tim thought as he drove, "I must have a dinner date or something I'm supposed to go to tonight." He thought hard, trying to remember. This concentration kept him from thinking about the Ark, for Tim did not forget dates or obligations.

Wally greeted Tim home with a, "Good evening, Mr. Sorsen. How was your day?"

"Don't ask, Wally!"

"I can imagine, Sir. I've been watching you and the Ark on TV. There's a special on right now if you'd care to watch it?"

"No thanks, Wally, I'm all Arked out!"

Chapter 3

"Lift up your hands toward the sanctuary; and bless the LORD" (*Psalms* 134:2).

Sunday morning, Tim and Wally walked into Sacred Heart of Jesus Church. Phil and Mary Simmons were greeting. "Good morning, Tim. Good morning, Wally. Did you bring the Ark with you?" Phil laughed at his own humor as only a big man like Phil could laugh–loud.

"Afraid not, Phil."

Mary said, "Tim, we're all so excited. You must tell us all about it. Will we get a chance to see it?"

"I don't know, Mary, you get the news as fast as I do. Everything will be on the tube when they decide what will become of it."

Fortunately people were coming in behind them, forcing Tim and Wally to continue on into the church. Tim was conscious of people looking at him. They sat down in chairs, as SHJ had no pews or kneelers, only padded chairs. The church was a modern building with no statues, only a large wooden cross above and behind the altar. It was in the shape of a half circle with the altar in the middle of the straight side. It had a large vaulted ceiling, rising from the sides to a long narrow cupola which had many clear glass windows and ran from the altar to the entrance. Behind the altar were very large elevated windows; behind the wooden cross was clear glass which gave one a view of the heavens.

Tim felt depressed and uncomfortable–unusual, because he always looked forward to Sunday and Mass. He tried hard to concentrate on prayer, without success. "Why am I so depressed and ashamed?" he thought. "Nothing has happened that should depress me, and I have done nothing I should be ashamed of!" He knew that the Ark was the source, but he did not know why.

Tim wondered if the finding of this chest was some sort of a sign to him and others who sometimes questioned the existence of God? He thought about his many years studying and memorizing his Catechism, the many Sundays listening to homilies explaining the word of God, and of the great faith and devotion of others. He was aware that his faith sometimes escaped him and that his devotion to SIMI left little time for God. Did this ancient symbol of God appear to retestify that, "I am," "I exist," or, "I am the way?" Was the path that he was traveling–very successfully–the wrong path? Aroused, he thought, "Hey, my life has been a benefit to mankind, I. . . ."

Tim's rationalization was interrupted by the commentator announcing that Father Eisenrich and Deacon Herzog would preside at the celebration. Tim remembered that he was to distribute Communion today as he was a Eucharistic Minister. Again something he enjoyed, but please not today! Maybe he just wouldn't go up . . . but no, everyone knew he was here.

Carl Cook was doing the reading. Carl was a good reader, but Tim was not listening. He was haunted by his experiences with the Ark at SIMI! Did he actually hear an answer to his question, "I would like to talk to you?" He knew he heard no sound yet he definitely knew he perceived an answer. Imaginary or not, the memory of it would not leave him. He stood for the reading of the Gospel.

Tim sat and with great determination listened to Father Eisenrich's homily.

"All of us are most aware of the news that the Ark of the Covenant possibly has been found. While this is a very important archeological find, its importance has been blown completely out of sight of its real significance!

"This chest was very meaningful to the ancient Israelites. If it's been found, then it's notable because it, along with thousands of other finds, support biblical history. Its value to us is no more than that!

"In trying to come up with a statement on this news event today, I found that Paul had already done it for me, approximately one thousand nine hundred years ago in his letter to the Hebrews. Please pay attention to this reading; it has a very important answer for you and me and people who might be asked about the value of this find to Christians and Jews.

"*Hebrews*, 9:1-14.

"*'The first covenant had regulations for worship and an earthly sanctuary. For a tabernacle was constructed, the outer one, in which were the lampstand, the table, and the showbread; this was called the holy place. Behind the second veil was the tabernacle called the holy of holies, in which were the golden altar of incense and the ark of the covenant entirely covered with gold. In the ark were the golden jar containing the manna, the rod of Aaron which had blossomed, and the tablets of the covenant. Above the ark were the cherubim of glory overshadowing the place of expiation.'*

"I interrupt Paul here to explain that the 'place of expiation' is where the blood of sacrificed animals is sprinkled for atonement.

"Paul continues, '*We cannot speak now of each of these in detail. These were the arrangements for worship. In performing their service the priests used to go into the outer tabernacle constantly, but only the high priest went into the inner one, and that but once a year, with the blood which he offered for himself and for the sins of the people. The Holy Spirit was showing thereby that while the first tabernacle was still standing, the way into the sanctuary had not yet been revealed. This is a symbol of the present time, in which gifts and sacrifices are offered that can never make perfect the conscience of the worshiper, but can only cleanse in matters of food and drink and various ritual washings: regulations concerning the flesh, imposed until the time of the new order.*'

"Those of you who have drifted off, please now pay attention!

"'*But when Christ came as high priest of the good things which have come to be, he entered once for all into the sanctuary, passing through the greater and more perfect tabernacle not made by hands, that is, not belonging to this creation. He entered, not with the blood of goats and calves, but with his own blood, and achieved eternal redemption. For if the blood of goats and bulls and the sprinkling of a heifer's ashes can sanctify those who are defiled so that their flesh is cleansed, how much more will the blood of Christ who through the eternal spirit offered himself up unblemished to God, cleanse our consciences from dead works to worship a living God!*'

"I would like to repeat, '*from dead works to worship a living God,*' for emphasis!

"Why don't we take a few silent moments and reflect on the insight of Paul."

During the Our Father, Tim held hands with Wally and the lady next to him who had a warm and nervous hand.

After the Sign of Peace, Tim went up to the altar and the tabernacle as he was to distribute the Body of Christ. He opened the tabernacle, genuflected, and removed the reserved Hosts. He then froze like Lot's wife, looking into the tabernacle lined with gold colored metal reflecting the lights, duplicating Tim's experience of looking into the empty Ark! "My God! My dear God! Was that what was in the Ark the first time it was opened?"

Fellow distributor Opal Snyder said, "Tim, are you all right?" Tim was oblivious of her.

Father took hold of his arm, closing his hand vise-like, to get his attention, saying, "You OK, Tim?"

"Yes, I am Father, excuse me." He placed the Hosts on the altar. As people accepted the Host, Tim said, "The Body of Christ," with great conviction.

As they left church, Farther Eisenrich, who was shaking hands with the parishioners, said to Tim, "By the way, the Senior Citizens' Bingo will be coming up the last of next month. Will you chair it again?"

"I'll be glad to, Father."

"Thanks, Tim."

"Thank you, Father!" Both knew the thank you was for Father not mentioning or commenting on the Ark and not about the chairmanship of the Seniors' Bingo.

Tim was sorry he did not ask Father for help by saying, "I'm very disturbed and need your help!" Instead he charted a course to the parking lot that would avoid as many people as possible.

Chapter 4

"For my thoughts are not your thoughts, nor are your ways my ways, says the LORD*" (Isaiah 55:8).*

Monday morning Tim started for work fortified by coffee, orange juice, and peanut butter toast, insisted on by Wally.

June greeted Tim both when he entered and again when he sat down to his desk. He noticed fresh flowers on his window ledge. June followed him into his office, pad in hand, to advise him of the latest happenings and of his agenda for the day.

Tim looked at June as she sat before him looking at her notes. June had a peaches and cream complexion and a sensual mouth. Her large wide-set blue eyes, full reddish-brown eyebrows, complimented her soft red, shoulder length hair. She wore a loose fitting gray business suit that could not hide the perfection the exposed legs suggested.

"My God, what a beautiful woman!" he thought—a thought he had many times during June's tenure with the company. He never once told her that he thought her beautiful or that he was attracted to her. He thought of telling her, but was afraid she would not be receptive, even though Tim knew that her marriage was an unhappy one. Her husband was a school teacher and spent all of his waking hours teaching or researching education. He spent very little time as a companion to June. Regardless, Tim knew she would remain loyal to her husband. He also knew his prideful ego could not take a no!

June looked up from her notes and said, "It seems that a great deal of work and communications were done this weekend by the government, Mr. Mills, and the Sales Department. It has been determined by the State Department and Mr. Mills that the shipment of the artifact did actually come from Israel, by way of Canada. They are crating it up this morning to ship it back to Israel."

"No! **No!** They can't ship it back!"

"But, Mr.Sorsen, it belongs to Israel. I know how you feel. I don't want them to ship it back either. It's a simple case of ownership. Besides, it's out of our hands. It's being handled by the US Government. They are going to spirit it away by helicopter before the media finds out. Mr. Bates asked us not to mention this to anyone."

Tim sat at his desk with his hands in a prayer-like position thinking, "Bates is right, this Thing does not belong to SIMI; it should have never been shipped here. SIMI is an international machine company, specializing in large construction machinery, not a collector of art."

Coming back to his own world, he said, "Thank you, June. What else do you have?"

"Not a great deal, Sir. SIMI has been going along on its own it seems. Mr. Mills wants to know if you would like to call a staff meeting to get the departments back running on 'all eight' as Mr. Mills puts it."

"Did Martin suggest a time?"

"He thought ten o'clock would be a good time for everyone if that time would be good for you."

"Please have Martin set it up."

"Yes, Sir."

"June, I have a few things to do, if you'll excuse me."

He had absolutely nothing to do except the work he had on his desk, which June had put there. He wanted to be alone, to think. "What does all this mean? What does all this mean to me?" He did not have the slightest glimmer to help him ease his frustrations. He needed help, someone with greater insights than his. "If only Mom were here." She was the most intelligent person he could think of. He never knew his Father. "Father—hey, that's it. I'll go see Father." Not his real father, but Father Blaine. Father, long-time pastor of Sacred Heart of Jesus, principal and religious teacher of SHJ High School, was like a real father to Tim. Father Blaine was retired now and was at St. John's Seminary where they had facilities for aging priests. Father was a brilliant man, who, Tim did not mind admitting, was more intelligent than he. It had been some time since he had visited Father. When he first retired, Tim visited him often. As time wore on, the intervals became longer. "It's been at least six months since I've seen Father John."

Speaking to his desk's intercom, he said, "June, will you please contact Martin and tell him to handle the staff meeting. I'm going to take the rest of the day off, to take care of some personal business."

"Yes, Sir," said June in surprise.

Before Tim left SIMI, he drove his Mercedes over to Receiving, jumped out, and went in to see the Ark one last time before it was shipped back to Israel.

He walked over to where they had the Ark only to be

disappointed. The Ark was all crated up and ready for shipment. He looked at the crate, thinking, "Maybe it's all right if they ship the Ark back. Maybe what was in the Ark is still here." Looking around him oblivious to the workers in the building, he thought, "I'll ask It if It's still here!" A prickly feeling started in the small of his back and traveled up to the back of his neck! He turned quickly and headed for the door. He started repeating to himself, "Ask It, ask It, ask It. You're afraid, You're afraid." He reached the door and his car and headed for St. John's.

Father John wasn't in his room. Tim checked in the little office in the front of the building where Father stayed. An elderly lady said, "You want to see Father John? Why does everybody want to see Father John? He must be selling drugs or something. I don't know where he is, but if I were to guess, I would say the library. He reads a lot."

"I forget, where is the library?"

"That building right over there that says 'Library' on the front," she said pointing.

Tim, red-faced, said, "Thank you."

He found Father John researching in three large books, all open on the table before him.

"Hello, Father John. How are you?"

"I'm fine and very busy. Oh, it's you, Tim. How are you? Long time, no see."

"I'm fine, Father. I'm sorry it's been so long, but I just couldn't seem to make the time."

"I understand. You always were very selfish and self-centered."

This did not bother Tim. He knew Father as very candid and deadly accurate with his analysis.

"Brought you your favorite cinnamon roll from Martha's."

"Great, I'll have it after what they call 'breakfast,' in the morning. Want to go outside and sit on a hard bench or go over to where they have my cell and find easy chairs?"

"You give me little choice, Father."

"Hand me my walker, Tim."

He hadn't noticed the walker behind Father.

"What's with the walker, Father? You have a fall or something?"

"I guess you could call it a fall—a fall from being old to being very old. I've had a very good life, and it's time I have a little discomfort. Life is not all cinnamon rolls. I've been blessed in comparison to Job and so many of my fellow men and women. You wouldn't know much about that. I bet it's been a long time since you've had your nose in a Bible, or a history book."

"Might surprise you to know that I attended Bible study classes at Sacred Heart of Jesus for several years."

"I'm glad that SHJ is still a parish that teaches and promotes Scripture," thought Father aloud.

It was a slow and painful walk to Father's dorm. Tim had time to study Father. His eighty-seven years looked more like ninety-seven. He was very thin, very wrinkled, and very bent. He had two great things left—the twinkle in his eyes, and his lovable smile, a perpetual smile from the many years as a parish priest or from an inner satisfaction gained from his knowledge.

They went into the sitting room on the front of the dorm. It covered the entire front of the building. It had four large plain windows on either side. The room was furnished with two couches and five overstuffed chairs, with none matching the other. There were three end tables of different styles, and three varying lamps and shades. On the polished hardwood floors were two large matching rugs.

After Father sat down, Tim took the walker and put it behind his chair. They sat and looked at each other, the floor, and back at each other for a few moments. These were not embarrassing moments. They were just enjoying each other's company as they had silently done so many times before.

"So, Tim, what's new in your life, or is it just business—business as usual?" said Father, twinkling and smiling a bit more than usual.

"You probably know more about what's been going on in my life than I do, unless that miserable old TV of yours has conked out." Tim knew he followed all current events by reading several newspapers and watching his little black and white TV, which Tim tried to replace with a color TV, but Father said he did not care what color their eyes were.

"Yes, I did see you on TV, and I did read about you and the Ark in the papers. I understand that they're not sure yet if it's the real Ark, and probably won't be sure for some time yet. Sounds like you've had a very exciting experience."

"Yes, exciting, but also disturbing."

"What do you mean, 'disturbing'?"

"Can't explain it, Father. Did you see or read about the effect the first opening of the Ark had on those who were present?"

"Yes, of course, I did."

"Would you know what caused this effect, Father?"

"Yes, of course, I know what caused the effect, but it is more important that you and the world know."

"Can't you please tell me?"

"No, Tim. It would do no good for me to tell you. You must reason it out for yourself. Then it won't be a matter of faith, but a matter of knowledge. You must desire to find out. Let me ask you, what do you think caused the effect?"

"I'm not sure, but I thought maybe there was something in the Ark that affected us."

"How perceptive."

"Are you making fun of me?"

"No, I'm saying you were perceptive of the fact that the only thing that happened in your building that could have affected everyone there was the opening of the Ark."

"But how could the mere opening of the Ark cause such an effect?"

"You're evading answering your own question. I will again ask what **you** think. What do you think was in the Ark, Tim?"

Father's bid of two in a suit, demanded an answer. Tim studied Father's face, inspected the floor between them. He then looked directly at Father, tears began welling in his eyes, his breath coming in short gasps, and, "Father, I think God was in the Ark," gushed out!

"How perceptive. I say this not to poke fun at you but in praise of your perceptiveness. It is not everybody who can perceive the presence of God!"

Tim listened attentively, not bothering to wipe the tears from his face.

"Yes, some three thousand years ago the ancient Israelites symbolically using God's Word and relics, put God in a box. The Ark containing the two tablets of stone, a vessel of manna, and the rod of Aaron, symbolized the presence of God.

"It is mentioned many times in your Bible, not only describing it, but telling what it meant to—and how it was used by—the ancient Israelites. Great idea when you think about it. Who could defeat an army who carried God with them? Who could defeat a nation who had God in a box? Later on they transferred God to a temple."

"But, Father, we are taught that God is everywhere!"

"Of course God is all-present. But He is only present when He is asked to be present by the ancient Israelites—or by you, Tim."

"That's cruel, Father. Why isn't God with me at all times?"

"Because your ways are not God's ways!"

"Father, I think my life has been pretty successful and productive."

"Tell me what you mean by successful."

"It's embarrassing to talk about myself, but I'm proud of the accomplishments, large and small, that I've made."

"What are these accomplishments, Tim?"

Tim shifted about in his chair, looking uncomfortable. He said, "Father you know my life as well as anybody. You know that I was an 'A' student in grade school, high school, and college. I also excelled in sports and was involved in student activities. You know that from a small five-employee dealership I built a multi-million dollar machine company that employs hundreds. The company has been featured in newspapers, magazines, and on television. I believe I am the driving force behind the company's success."

"Hey, Tim, didn't those five employees help you a little bit? Also don't the hundreds of employees do something toward the success of the company?"

Tim looked down and studied the weave in the material of his slacks.

"Do you think God gives you credit for these accomplishments, Tim?"

"I certainly hope so! The company is a benefit to hundreds of employees. It also benefits this city, county, state, and even the world at large. The company and I donate thousands to charity."

"Tim, we both know that the charity donations were used for tax write-offs and public relations. I know you well, Timothy Sorsen, and you never did anything for anybody without exacting some sort of payment. Ask yourself this question, which I do not need to know the answer to, but to which you need to know the answer: Did you make these accomplishments for God, your employees, the state, the world at large, or recognition and fortune? Intent is the key here.

"Remember the formula I once taught you? NG stands for no good. Now NG isn't bad, it just lacks good, so it equals zero. G stands for good and equals one. A person can live their whole life without doing anything bad and still not gain any points, using this formula. Let's say that I own a logging company which puts logs in a river to get them to a market downstream. One day a drowning man finds one of my logs and it saves his life. I am no hero, Tim. My only gain would be the money I received from the sale of the log, which was my intent when I had the log placed in the water. I get the price of the log and a zero!

"Have you ever seen Jesus in one of your employees, in some friend or neighbor?"

"No, of course not. That's just a figure of speech, isn't it, seeing Jesus in someone?"

"Do you see what you've done, Tim? You've placed God in the sanctuary of the church, possibly even in the tabernacle. Consider the ancient Israelites. They thought, like you, that they had God in a safe place. They could go get Him, use Him, when they wanted Him. Now, they wouldn't want God with them all the time—when they sold a lame donkey to their neighbor, when they beat their slaves, or when they went out drinking and story-telling with their friends."

"Do we have that much power over God that we can have Him leave us and then call for Him at will?"

"No, Tim, we have no power over God! He has given us a free will. If we choose to dismiss God entirely, He is dismissed from our earthly life. If we choose to proclaim Him on Sunday and dismiss Him on weekdays, He allows this. It is a great pitfall for us because God is all aware of all our thoughts and deeds, whether it be on a Sunday or on a Monday, whether it be in a church, tavern, or brothel."

"How do I keep God with me in my daily life, Father?"

"Simply ask Him to be with you, and be aware of His presence in you, the people you work with, play with, and pray with! Let me warn you, as you have heard others warned, 'Be careful what you ask for, you might get it!' Many have found that God is a pain in the neck."

"How so, Father?"

"Well, God and man do not think alike. What pleases man does not always please God, and what pleases God does not always please man. If you have time in your busy life tonight, find a place of solitude and imagine how it would affect your life if God were your constant companion. He would share your most intimate thoughts, observe your every deed and hear your every word!

"If you made such an invitation to God, you would need to think thoughts that would please God, do deeds to please Him, and speak words that would please Him! Of course, you would need or have the help of God's grace to make this possible.

"What you really need to do, Tim, is have a good talk with God."

"Oh sure, Father. I'll just sit right here and talk to God."

"That's right, it's as easy as that. It takes some practice at first. Remember God speaks to you through your mind using your intelligence, for you would not understand His. Would you like to talk to God, Tim?"

"Of course, I would."

"OK. Again you must find some time in your busy life and a place of solitude, bow your head and assume a prayer-like attitude and simply think, 'I would like to talk to you, dear God.'"

Tim jumped to his feet and went over to the window and looked out. He continued looking out, seeing nothing but the side of another building. From his response, Father perceived that he was disturbed about talking to God. Neither man spoke for several minutes.

Continuing to look out the window, Tim said, "I didn't tell you about what happened when I was alone with the Ark after everyone had left. I went back by myself to the Receiving Department. I sat looking at the Ark, thinking that if there had been something in the Ark, maybe it was still in the building. I don't know what possessed me, but I looked up and said, 'I would like to talk to you.' Father. . . ." Tim's voice broke. It took moments for him to gather himself to say, "Father, It said, *'What do you want to talk about, my son?'*"

Again there was silence between the two men, with Father contemplating the back of his hands and Tim looking out the window at the nether scene.

Finally, Father asked, "Did you tell 'It' what you wanted to talk about?"

"No, I was afraid. I'm not even sure I heard It, sensed It, or imagined It. No, that's not right, I'm sure I received an answer, but I don't know how!"

"Did you see anything, Tim?"

"No."

"Then you did not have a Theophany."

"What is a Theophany?"

"Tim, I suggest you do some research on the Ark. And while you're at it, look up 'Theophany.' Until you can put a name on 'It,' until you can identify 'It,' you won't be able to find any answers."

"Father, do you have any answers for me? What do you make of all of this?"

"It was a message to the world, an invitation. This message has been given to the Israelites and the world many times before."

"What is the message, Father?"

"If you didn't perceive the message, I can't give it to you. But don't feel bad, Tim. From what I've seen on TV and read in the papers, the rest of the world didn't get the message either. Now if you want to find out what the message was, then answer 'It' and tell 'It' what you want to talk about. Come with me."

Father rose and motioned toward his walker. It again was a slow walk to their destination but was a much shorter walk. They were in the very small chapel of the dormitory. Father put aside his walker and went up to the tabernacle. Father opened the tabernacle, genuflected, fully touching the floor with his knee. Tim was surprised that this frail and feeble man was able to do this.

Rising, he picked up a match box kept by the tabernacle to light candles. He opened the box, dumped out its few matches. Using both hands, Father put the box into the tabernacle. Tim could not see his hands or the box. When he brought the box out, it was closed. Father again genuflected and closed the tabernacle. He turned, took his walker, and left the chapel, slowly making his way to his "cell."

"Tim, please sit in my big chair. I'll prop myself up on

the bed with some pillows. I'm more comfortable that way." He left his walker in the corner and went over to his small desk, opened a drawer, rummaged through it until he found some tape. Carefully he took two small pieces of tape and sealed the ends of the match box. He handed the box to Tim and made his way over to the bed. It took him a little time to arrange his pillows and get settled.

"Listen to me, Tim. You know me as a serious person, a person who doesn't believe in the mystical. I know you respect my knowledge, so I'm going to ask you to believe me when I say that I put God in that match box! I know you cannot imagine or contemplate this. Follow my previous advice and research, and meditate on and about the Ark, and you will understand. Do not under any circumstances open the match box. You are not ready to have God with you at all times. Do not question me on this, Tim. I know you! The box will help you center on your quest."

Father John, comfortably propped up on his bed, started tracing a flower pattern on the bedspread with his point finger. His thick ivory colored nail traced the outside of a rose and stopped at its center as if marking his place. "Tim, why are you so embarrassed to say you talked to God?"

Father started tracing again from the center of the flower patiently, for he knew Tim would take some time in researching and constructing his answer.

Tim, bending forward with his elbows on the arms of the easy chair, looking between his knees, studied the stitching on his left Florsheim. He looked up at Father and watched him trace the flower then looked back at the right shoe to complete the study of his shoes' sewn seams.

Still looking at his shoe, he said, "Father, I've read and heard about people who have had visions, talked to our Holy Mother, and God, for as long as I can remember."

Raising his head and looking directly at Father, he continued, "Frankly, Father, although I never told anyone, I thought they were cuckcoos! It seems they were always simple-minded, of no great intellect, people looking for attention."

With a quick-reaction chuckle and smile that wrinkled the corners of his eyes, Father shot back, "Well then, it seems you are slightly daft and not as smart as you thought you were!"

"That thought has crossed my mind, Father."

The venerable priest drew a circle around the rose as if to mark it traced. Looking at Tim, he said, "Let's talk about talking to God."

"I would like that, Father."

"Tim, most people talk to God every day without ever being aware that they are making such a communion! They often call it, 'talking to myself.' Think about talking to yourself, Tim. It is impossible to talk to oneself! You would need two intellects to exchange any thoughts. In other words, you cannot tell yourself anything you do not already know.

"Yes, it does seem like we're talking to ourselves because we think in a language. The same language we speak. The truth is, we review our intellect, that vast amount of information which we have read, heard, or learned from experience. All of this data is stored in our speaking language. So when we talk to ourselves, we are actually conversing with the source of that data which applies to our thought. A response comes back to us exactly like it does when we talk to another person. The only difference is there is no sound.

"How then do we talk to the source of our wisdom? Practically everyone has been told by their mother or guardian, 'make sure you have clean underwear on in case you are in an accident.'"

Tim shifted in his chair and smiled knowingly.

Father continued, "It was your mother's intention for you to use this good sense, not only at that moment, but always. I know your mother is dead, Tim. This, however, is still a direct communication from her, without the sound of her voice. I often think of my mother's sagacities spoken to me. I can even see her shaking her finger at me while schooling my common sense. So, if I tell you that I talked to my mother just now, it would be true, in essence!"

Father John paused, waiting for any comments Tim would have. He merely looked at Father, showing great interest in what he was saying.

"Now, God has given us such a great wealth of wisdom, directly and through the prophets, that we note the sound of His voice. He no longer has to appear in fire and smoke. Remember that those to whom He did speak had no way of knowing the wisdom that is available to us. Our cup runs over with His wisdom. He has said all that is necessary for us to hear. We can communicate endlessly with His wisdom!

"Experiment, ask God a simple question: 'Dear God, is it wrong to commit adultery?' His answer will come snapping back without hesitation. You learn to recognize God's communications. If the answer has to be analyzed and debated in the mind then this is your own thought process working. Also, be careful, Lucifer sometimes gets in on the act!"

Like a student, Tim raised his hand to interrupt, saying, "Why should I ask Him a question if I already know the answer?"

"Tim, most questions are those asked by people who

already know the answer, have the correct response at their finger tips, or in their data banks. Example: I just asked you why you were embarrassed about talking to God. It took you a long time to answer. I knew it would. You said you thought that people who claim they have done this were cuckoo. I knew you would. Review most conversations you have with people and you will find that with most of the questions that you asked, you already knew the answer. You can of course fill in the gaps in your wisdom from others' wisdom. This then makes them a source. Some people can communicate with others without much exchange. Lovers who know each other are a good example. You could fill volumes with their silent communications.

"Talking to God should not embarrass you. You should be elated and awed."

"But I don't know what He's saying to me, Father!"

"It is somewhere in your mind, or you can research it from God's word. It is your communiqué, Tim. Would you like a glass of altar wine, this year's vintage?"

"Yes, please."

"It's in the bottom desk drawer. Will you pour?"

Tim found the wine and two water glasses. They concluded their evening without referring to the Ark, the match box, or heavenly dialogues, chatting about health and politics.

Chapter 5

"So I say to you, 'ask and you shall receive; seek and you shall find; knock and the door will be opened to you" (*Luke* 11:9).

Tim arrived at SIMI at 8:02 a.m. June greeted him very cheerfully, not showing her surprise that he was an hour early. After Tim entered his own office, June came in to advise him of the schedule for the day. "You've set today aside to review with Mr. Mills and his staff all current contracts."

"June, has the . . . ah . . . you know . . . the Ark been shipped back to Israel?"

"I'm not sure, Sir, but it's left SIMI. An Air Force helicopter flew it out yesterday. We were not told its destination. Our bill of lading shows we delivered it to the United States Air Force."

"Well then, this Ark thing is over, right June?"

"I sure hope so, Mr. Sorsen!"

"Is Martin in?"

"I don't believe so. He usually comes in about nine."

"OK, I'll wait for him. Anyway, it looks like you have some work for me on the desk."

"Yes, Sir. Those are completed contract sales with their

cost analyses."

"Good, it will seem good to get back to work. Tell Martin to set up our meeting and advise me of the time."

"Yes, Sir. There's fresh coffee in your thermo."

"Thanks, June," he said, as she left him to his work.

He opened the first file folder marked, "Caterpillar Tractor Co. and The City of Louisville, Kentucky." He stared at the cover sheet, but nothing registered. He continued to stare until he shook himself loose from his trance. "What the hell is wrong with me?" he thought. He reminded himself that these analyses were of the utmost importance to SIMI. If he was not aware of the current cost, the company might accrue deficits from which it could not recover, or, without his awareness, could price the company out of the market.

Why was he thinking like this? He was talking down to himself as Father John did to him yesterday–preaching to himself common business practices.

He hadn't thought about that, but Father John did talk down to him yesterday–treating him like a small child, putting God in a match box, and telling him he was not ready to have God with him at all times. He thought, "I'll give Father a scolding next time I see him. I'll ask him why I'm not ready to have God with me at all times. What makes him think I don't already have God with me?"

He reflected for a moment and thought, "Maybe I don't have God with me at all times. I seldom think about Him during the week. What did Father say about having God with me at all times? 'All you do is just ask It.' Do you suppose 'It' is still here at SIMI and that 'It' is God?!"

Again he felt his neck prickle. He shivered and stood up from his desk and went to the window overlooking SIMI.

He never noticed before, but he could see the Receiving building. He stared at the building without any particular thought pattern. Still staring at the building, Tim said, without sound, "Are You still here?" There was no reply! "Father said, 'Put a name on It.' Are You still here, God?"

"Yes, Tim, I am here."

He was surprised that he did not feel any fear as before. In place of fear he felt comfort. Yes, he could feel God's presence, and It gave him great comfort! As was Tim's nature, he paused to analyze. First, he had not heard an actual sound. In fact, there was no sound. Second, it could be his imagination or his conscience, which very often talks to him.

"Are You my conscience?"

The answer was, *"I have been called many things conscience, spirit, moon, sun, fire, smoke, thunder, and lighting, but I belong to you and you belong to me."*

Tears welled in his eyes, and he began to breathe in short gasps. Martin came through the side door to his office saying, "Good morning, earlybird, here's your worm."

Tim whirled shouting, "Martin, I'm in conference right now!"

"Hey, Tim, I checked with June, and she said you were alone. I'm sorry," he said, looking around the office and back to Tim's tearful face.

Both men stood looking at each other for a moment. Martin ventured, "Are you all right; is anything the matter?"

"Yes, there is, Martin! Please come in, and I'm sorry for yelling at you. It's this Ark thing. I'm afraid I've let it get to me."

"Oh hell, that's all over. You know what they say, 'Today's joke is yesterday's problem.'"

"I don't mean the problems the Ark caused; it's the Ark itself that's bothering me."

"Hey, Tim, lighten up. A lot of the experts don't even think that was the real Ark."

"Well, I don't know if it's the Ark or maybe that I need some R and R. Whichever the case, I'm so mixed up I can't think straight!"

"I didn't think anything could mix you up, Tim."

"Well, this has, and I think I'll take some time off. First thing I'm going to do is check in with Dr. Phillips for a complete physical. Then, maybe I'll take a short trip somewhere."

"Now you're talking sense; you carry a big load around here! Get away for a few and you'll be as good as new. You'll be back, living up to what some of the employees call you, "SIMI's Pit Bull."

"I'm counting on you, Martin, to oversee this company while I'm gone. Work with June, and she'll advise you of what's on my agenda."

"You're starting to worry even before you start your trip! Relax, we'll do fine and look forward to your return—refreshed, and full of piss and vinegar. I don't suppose you want to review contracts today?"

"No, will you and your staff handle them?"

"Of course, when are you planning on leaving?"

"As soon as I can get out of here. You're welcome to use my office whenever you need."

"Thanks."

"On your way out, send June in, please."

"Enjoy yourself, Tim. Relax, and not to worry."

"Thanks, Martin."

Tim spent over an hour with June making arrangements for his contemplated absence. She was able to wangle a 9:00 a.m. appointment, through a cancellation, with Dr. Phillips. She also was going to check on several possible trips with travel agencies and advise Tim at home, tomorrow.

Tim lay on his side completely nude on a white paper-covered table while Dr. Phillips checked his prostate. When the examination was over, the doctor said, "That does it, Tim. Why don't you go ahead and get dressed and come into my office, and we'll put the results of all this poking and blood-letting together."

"Tell me, what prompted this visit, Tim? Have you had any problems? . . . chest pains, shortness of breath, or dizziness?"

"No, Carl. I just felt a little out of sorts."

"What do you mean 'out of sorts'?"

"Can't really put my finger on it, just out of sorts and sometimes confused."

"You have to consider that you are now sixty-two years old and can expect that your body is going through changes. You'll feel these changes from now on.

"I found nothing in my examination that tells me you're not going to live a long life. I did find a couple of things I'd like to follow up on with further exams. You haven't had a stress test in the last three years. Your heart seems to be working a little extra hard, even though your pressures are normal.

"We won't get the results of the blood tests back until tomorrow. If there's anything you should know about these, I'll call you.

"One thing I'd like to warn you about is stress. I'm sure in your line of work there's a lot of stress. Now this may surprise you hearing a doctor admit it, but we really don't know much about stress. I know some doctors do claim to know about the effects of stress, but they have a head full of rancid rhubarb. There's only one thing we know for sure and that's that it has a negative effect on the body and the mind!

"My advice to you, Timothy, is to extend your vacation from one week to two weeks or a month. After all, money isn't everything."

"Listen to who's talking!"

"Get out of here, Tim. If you didn't have stress when you came in, you will when you get my bill!"

On his trip home from the doctor, Tim had an urge to go to church. "Crazy, it's Tuesday, it's 10:30 a.m.!" But the urge was strong and would not succumb to the rationalization of the day and time. On the other side, his urge suggested, "Why not? You're on vacation. A visit to church will be relaxing."

He didn't want to go to Sacred Heart of Jesus because Father and the church secretary would want to know why he was there. He turned the Mercedes around and headed north to the Forest Lake area and Our Lady of the Forest Church. He went up to the doors of the church but found them locked. A voice from behind him said, "I'm sorry, the church is locked. May I help you?" Tim turned to find a little priest who looked as old as religion itself.

"I just wanted to visit church, Father."

"You can go in through the office if you'd like. We keep the doors locked to discourage vandals." They both started walking toward the office attached to the side of the church.

"Do you need counsel, or would you like to talk to someone?"

"Surprising himself with his own honesty, he replied, "I would like to talk to God."

"Oh, how wonderful it is to hear someone say that! I think that will please Him very much because there are not a lot of people talking to God these days!"

Father ushered him through the door and pointed to the access to the church. "Visit as long as you like. You can leave by the front doors. The church doors will lock behind you."

"The church doors will lock behind you.... The church doors will lock behind you...," ran through Tim's mind, bringing to mind all this talk about putting God in an Ark, a temple, a church—yes, even a box. "God is all powerful; no one can lock God in anywhere," thought Tim! "Father John did say that man could lock God out with their free will." He wasn't sure he understood Father's meaning.

Our Lady of the Forest was a beautiful older church. It was so churchy that it made one want to whisper and tip-toe. It had a white marble altar rail in front of a white marble altar. Behind the altar was a very ornate white marble arch around a stained glass window depicting Mary. Below the window was a small white altar above which was a gold door to the tabernacle. On either side of the church were lifelike statues of the Sacred Heart of Jesus and the Holy Mother.

Tim found a front pew and knelt down, crossing himself. He looked up at a statue of the Blessed Mother and said an Act of Contrition. He kept looking at the statue, thinking that he wasn't here to talk to the Holy Mother. He was here to talk to God. He got up from his pew and crossed over to the other side of the church and knelt before the statue of Jesus. He instantly felt foolish and ashamed for his actions and started to say Hail Marys to cover any disrespect he may have shown Mary.

Tim sat back in his pew and tried to relax his mind and body. What was all of this that was going on with his mind? He stared at the statue of the Sacred Heart of Jesus, which stared back holding one hand over His heart and extending His other hand toward Tim.

He spoke with his thoughts to the Person represented by the beautiful image before him made of plaster and oil paint. "You are all powerful! If You can speak to me, then it would be simple for You to give me a sign, any sign. Move Your fingers, blink Your eyes. Tim found himself clenching his teeth, his body taut, trying physically and mentally to force the work of man to give him a sign from God.

He bowed his head, putting his face in his hands in shame for these thoughts, void of any wisdom. His head came upright. "Wisdom, that's the answer!" Wisdom had always been his answer to any problem he had ever had. Whenever he came to a roadblock in his life, he would remove the impediment with wisdom.

Where would he gain this wisdom? Again he thought of Father John. He could pick Father's mind, or better still, he could do some research as Father suggested. He left church refreshed, with determined strides.

Tim called June at 8:05 the next morning to advise her that he had decided against any trip. She was disappointed because she had found several exciting "getaway" trips. He thanked her for her efforts and told her he was still going to take some time off to do some research. "Keep the place running while I'm gone. I'll call you in a week or ten."

"Enjoy yourself and relax, Mr. Sorsen."

"Thanks, June."

Wally came downstairs saying, "Here you are, Mr.

Sorsen, I found this tablet suitable for making notes. You can use this pencil I keep by the phone in the hall."

"Thanks, Wally. I'll be back for lunch."

"Anything particular you'd like, Sir?"

"Yes, got any of your famous ham salad?"

"I'll be glad to make some up for you, Sir. I have some honey-baked ham."

"Great, Wally. How about stuffed tomatoes? Make two. You and I haven't had a weekday lunch together in a long time."

Tim found a wealth of information on the Ark—a great deal of historical and religious data relating to the Ark. He noted that "Ark" is derived from Latin, "arca," meaning "container" or "box". There were two Hebrew words to describe an Ark: "tebah" and "aron." "Tebah" is a rectangular building that can float like Noah's Ark, also a box that can float, like the box of papyrus in which the infant Moses was placed.

"Aron," refers to an Egyptian coffin used to bring Joseph's body from Egypt to Shechem. The body was placed in the coffin in a fetal position. Hence its size would be about the size of the Ark in question.

"Aron," also was known as a wooden chest with a hole in its lid for collecting money. Tim made notes that "Aron" was referred to some 200 times in the Old Testament as a holy vessel connected with the presence of God. An important difference showed in the titles given the Ark to show different concepts of what the Ark represented:

"The Ark of God,"
"The Ark of the God of Israel,"
"The Ark of the Lord,"
"The Ark of the Covenant of the Lord,"
"The Ark of the Testimony."

He was surprised to find that there are many claims about the final resting place of the Ark. Biblical history has it hidden in a cave never to be found again. Several churches claim to have the Ark; some have their claim on display. Some stories of how the Ark came into their possession are feasible; some are not.

Tim found that most biblical scholars believe that the Ark was hidden from Israel's enemies and has never been found.

He also found that the Bible states that two Cherubim were carved in the doors of Solomon's temple. This suggested to Tim, at least in part, that the temple and the Ark were to be used for the same purpose.

On his way home he stopped at the "Worn Cover Book Store" and bought two new Bibles, a "New American," revised edition and a "Jerusalem Bible" along with a large dictionary of the Bible.

"Wally, I'm enjoying my day very much. Thank you for having lunch with me, and thank you for these delicious looking stuffed tomatoes! You know you should go into business and package and sell your ham salad."

Pleased, Wally replied, "Oh, I'm sure there are a lot of people who have the same recipe."

"Wally, what do you know about the Bible?"

"Very little, Sir. My only association with the Bible is listening to the readings in church. I don't understand most of the readings, only Father's interpretations. That's when I listen."

"You and I are in the same boat. I bought a couple of Bibles today and a dictionary to do some studying of the Bible."

"I think that's great. You need some interest in your life besides your work."

"What I'm really interested in is finding out why the Ark affected everyone present at Its first opening. I'm afraid I won't rest until I do!"

"I'm happy to find out that this bothers you, too, Sir. I was beginning to think that I'd gone off the deep end about the Ark. I've spent hours at night and most of the last few days thinking about the Ark and what it all meant."

"Tell me about your thoughts, Wally. Did you come to any conclusions?"

"Well, not conclusions, but maybe some plausible answers. I'm kind of embarrassed to talk about them. But, I think God was the One who affected everyone at the first opening of the Ark. I think God was giving us all a message!"

Wally, who was not much of a talker and very hard to get into a conversation, went on as if driven. "God does not force Himself on anyone. But maybe this time He made His presence known to say, 'I am not in that chest anymore than I am here with you.' He told us that He is, was, and always will be everywhere. He wants us to be more conscious of His presence. He does not want to be kept pressed between the pages of our Bibles or in an Ark.

"He said, *'I am here,'*" Wally exclaimed, stabbing the air beside his chair with his point finger! "I think God said that we are all wrong in our relationships with Him! We should be more intimate and constantly aware of His presence. I. . . ." Wally stopped suddenly, embarrassed at his outpouring, for he noticed that Tim had stopped eating, put down his fork, and placed his hands in his lap, head bent staring at his half-eaten stuffed tomato, listening intently.

"I'm sorry, Sir. I know this sounds strange to you!"

"No! No! **No!**" Tim responded, sensing Wally's embarrassment. "I'm as embarrassed as you are by my own thoughts about the Ark, and they're not far removed from yours. What you've said may be a profound reality. You have a greater insight and sharper focus than I."

Wally remained silent, cleaning the dishes from the table, taking Tim's half-eaten lunch away. Tim was going to stop him because he was still hungry, but didn't want to embarrass him any further. He jumped up and helped Wally scrape the dishes and put them into the dishwasher.

Intentionally changing the subject and knowing Wally's love of baseball, Tim said, "Hey, Wally, how's your newfound love, the Colorado Rockies, coming? Any chance for that ragtailed outfit?"

"Wouldn't you like to have a piece of that club?"

"You're right there. With that kind of attendance, I'd be able to give you a raise.

"Wally, I'm going to spend some time in the study. Would you hold the calls?"

"Like, 'Mr. Sorsen cannot come to the phone,' or 'Mr. Sorsen is out'?"

"'Out,' sounds good Wally."

Tim spent a frustrating two hours in the study trying to pick from his Bibles, encyclopedias, and Bible dictionary wisdom and knowledge about God's relationship with man, and how He communicated with man. He could not get a handle on anything. He did find "Theophany" in the dictionary. Father John had said he hadn't had a Theophany. Theophany is face-to-face meeting with God. He felt flushed, thinking, "I didn't say I had a face-to-face meeting with God. I didn't suggest I had a meeting with God at all!" He reflected for a moment. "I did say I talked to 'It' and that I thought 'It' was God."

Completely baffled, he left the study and found Wally. "I'm going back to the book store."

"You read all those books already?"

"Wally, you're not only a great cook, but also a great comedian."

"If I could make a suggestion, Sir. I looked up the address of a religious book store that may have some books more pertinent. It is Carlsons at 925 South Adams Street, across from Empire Ford."

"Good thinking. I remember the store; I bought books there when I was in Bible study."

Tim was again confounded, reading covers and leafing through self-help books on how to read the Bible, understanding the Bible, and guides to reading the Bible.

Later, he was standing in front of the cashier, explaining what type of book he was looking for. He didn't want books that interpret the Bible for the reader, but one that tells the reader how to interpret it. "You know, a simple one for everyday Bible readers."

A priest, who looked like Jack Lemmon, was standing with two books in hand, waiting to pay. He said, "Sir, if I were a policeman, I'd give you a ticket for speeding! The book you described has never been written. There are probably several pamphlets that tell you in simple terms how to read the Bible. Yes, some of the guidelines are simple, but following the guidelines are not simple and require a lot of effort. A most important guideline for you would be to know your author! Find out what the Author's world was like. When did He write? Who were His friends? Who were His enemies? Then His message in Scripture will stand out to you."

"There is one book that comes close to the book you

described, and I'm sure they have it here." The priest jotted the title and author on a scrap of paper he found on the check-out counter, and handed it to Tim. "Hope I didn't talk you out of buying a bunch of books."

"No, Father, and I do appreciate your advice."

Tim returned to examining books and found the one the priest recommended. Leafing through the book, he thought. "This is exactly the book I need!" He purchased the book and headed home. By now he realized that his search and research were not simple ones and were going to take months–maybe years. Also it had been a long time since he had done any formal studying.

Tim returned home, greeted Wally, saying, "I think I'll rest a bit."

"Would you like me to turn down the bed, Sir?"

"No, no, I'll just sit in my chair and relax a bit."

"Is 7:30 all right for dinner?"

"Fine, Wally."

Tim went to his bedroom. What he really wanted was to be alone and away from all influences. It was as if he had a secret plan he hadn't even told himself about.

He sat in his reading chair. He still had the sack in his hand. He took the book out of the sack and put the sack on the end table and the book on top of the sack without opening the book. He thought, "I don't have time to start a formal study program. The simplest answer for me is to forget all this nonsense!"

His secret plan started slowly to seep into his mind. This was the reason he came to his bedroom for seclusion. Father John had said, "Give 'It' a name and tell 'It' what you want to talk about." Tim felt foolish. Why was he sidestepping his own mind? Why didn't he face the reality of his own mind? He knew he believed it was God.

He got out of his chair and knelt beside his bed. He said an Act of Contrition, an Our Father and started to say Hail Mary, when he mentally shouted to himself, "Hey, Tim, why are you playing 'Ring around the Rosary'?" At once he felt remorse, knowing that the Rosary was important, too. But this is not the approach he felt driven to take right now. He continued questioning himself. "Why are you avoiding talking to God? He has clearly answered you!"

His mind went blank. It was as if he were rebooting a computer to accept a new program. He put his face in his hands and thought, "I would like to talk to You."

There was no answer.

"Have I offended You by asking this?"

"I am sure you know that I would not be offended by such a request."

"I am very confused!"

"I am aware of your confusion."

"Were You in the Ark the first time it was opened?"

"There is no space where I am not present."

"But nothing happened the second time it was opened."

"Everything was the same the second time and is the same now except your awareness."

"Is it Your message that You are everywhere?"

"Only to those who can hear."

"Why did You choose to give me Your message?"

"I did not choose you. My message was for those that could hear, and you heard."

"What is it You want me to do?"

"Consider we are in communion today. What of tomorrow?"

Tim heard a very timid tap on his door and Wally's soft but excited voice saying, "Mr. Sorsen? Mr. Sorsen,

I'm very sorry to disturb you, but something very important is happening on the television. It's about the Ark. I thought you'd want to watch it! You can watch it in there on your TV if you'd like."

Tim hesitated, confused. Should he excuse himself and talk to Wally? Feeling foolish, he crossed himself and said, "I'll be right there, Wally."

He went into the bathroom and dashed cold water on his face and quickly dried with a towel.

Wally was in the den. Actually they did not know what to call the room—the library, the family room, or the den? It had two walls of books, a billiard table, large screen TV, leather couch, and two overstuffed leather chairs. Besides their bedrooms, Tim and Wally spent most all their time in the house in either the kitchen or the den.

"What channel is this, Wally?"

"It's NBC, but it's on all the networks. Would you prefer another?"

"No, this is fine."

Very fitting for Tim's arrival, the news commentator was saying: "For those of you just joining us, this is NBC's news coverage of the mysterious travels of the infamous Ark of the Covenant. It seems the Ark has disappeared into the nether world. Let's trace its travels as we know them and then go to that which we do not know.

"First of all, the Ark was shipped by Israel via Canada to Sorsen's International Machine Incorporated, by mistake. You are all aware of the controversy about the shipment and who was the rightful owner of the Ark. Then SIMI, the Israeli government, the Canadian government, and the United States government got the tangle straightened out. We now pick up the trail.

"The Ark was air-lifted from SIMI by a US Army helicopter to O'Hare Field in Chicago. It was received there by Israeli airlines and members of the Israeli government. As you would expect, there was all manner of security, both by the US and the Israeli governments, and now by the Israeli Airlines who are a model to all the airlines of the world on security.

"We do not have a departure time but believe it to be between 5:00 and 6:00 this morning. The plane, a C-10 cargo plane, was tracked across the United States to the New Jersey coast. It was picked up there by Greenland when it identified to stateside air control. When it passed over Greenland and was asked to identify, there was no response. Several attempts were made by the Greenland Air Control to contact the cargo plane without results.

"Air control in the Azores was contacted, who by now had the now unidentified cargo plane on their radar screen. Air controller Franz Helms, who was watching the plane's progress, took his eyes off of the screen for a split second to reach for his log book, looked back, and the plane was gone! Gone without a trace!

"Let's ask our guest via satellite, Mr. Wayne Johnston, Chief of Operations for the FAA: Mr. Johnston, why is the term used, 'without a trace'?"

"This is because when the plane disappeared from the radar screen it was close enough that the air controller would have seen falling debris or would have been able to see the plane falling. In other words, we would have been able to see if any catastrophe happened. There was no such evidence reported."

"Couldn't this have happened when Air Controller Helms was getting his log book?"

"Not likely. Helms took his eyes off of the screen for

69

only a few seconds. A plane in trouble would take several full minutes to fall from 36,000 feet. Even debris would take some time to fall seven miles!"

"Mr. Johnston, what do you think happened to the Israeli cargo plane?"

"You might as well ask one of your cameramen as me, for, with all that I have to work with at this moment, I don't have a clue. When we get more data, find the plane, find the plane's black box, then maybe we'll have some answers!"

"Thank you, Mr. Johnston. We will be back with you in a moment.

"Now, from his apartment at St. Michael's Basilica, we have Bishop Jerome of the Roman Catholic Church. Bishop, if this indeed is the true Ark of the Covenant that has been lost, will this loss be a great loss to the people of the world?"

"I do not consider the loss of the Ark as important as the loss of fervor that the finding of the Ark and the having of the Ark with us has caused. For us to have such fervor in our search for God is as it should be. I only hope this great passion does not disappear with the loss of the Ark!"

"Bishop, some say that there may be a message to us in the appearance of the Ark…?"

"I would think that this is probably true, but the Church will have to reflect much on this happening to fathom the message. My advice at this time would be for you to question the cameraman that Mr. Johnston referred to."

A smiling commentator said, "It seems we have a prophet here at NBC. We will take a short break and try to find our cameraman who is a prophet. Thank you, Bishop Jerome. NBC will continue its coverage of the missing Israeli cargo plane and its precious cargo after these messages."

During the commercials Tim and Wally glanced at each other, silently communicating their wonderment at what they were hearing. After several minutes of dramatized "buy this or you will not belong" scenes and compelling sounds, the NBC News reappeared.

The commentator summarized the news of the lost Ark to the moment. He then asked Mr. Wayne Johnston of the FAA, "Mr. Johnston, is there any possibility that this could be an act of terrorism?"

"If this turns out that there's a catastrophe, then, yes, it's a possibility. Its demise or capture would be a great coup for certain terrorist groups."

"Is there any sign that this was an act of terrorism?"

"I must point out again that we have nothing at this time as a sign of anything! In all seriousness, I would venture that maybe this is a sign in itself."

"What do you mean, 'a sign'?"

"I can only speak for myself, but it is a sign, to me, that something has happened that I do not understand."

"I think you spoke for all of us. Thank you, Mr. Johnston."

"My pleasure."

Tim stood up and said, "You can watch the rest, Wally."

"No," Wally said, and, like "Captain Kirk," took his remote and killed the TV. Tim was more at ease with the TV off and sat back down.

"What do you think of all of this, Sir?"

"I'm completely blank, Wally."

They both sat in silence, again communicating their wonderment to each other, perhaps like higher forms of intelligence would do.

"Wally, the one from the FAA, Johnston, mentioned 'sign.' I think maybe all of this is a sign."

"God only knows, Sir."

"No, no, Wally, I think part of the sign is that God wants us to know–to know something that's very important to Him!"

They relaxed for a moment. Wally said, "Tea, Sir?"

"Yes, please."

He returned with the tea. They sat in silence, each meditating about their God without guided direction. After a length of time that neither were aware of, Wally arose and took the cups to the kitchen.

Both men felt enervated, feeling good about their meditations, for both knew that God, Who is so beautiful and pure, welcomes examination.

Tim retired to his room and went directly to his night stand. He opened the drawer, took out the match box Father had given him along with a small pearl handle pen knife. Unceremoniously he cut the tape on both ends and replaced the knife in the drawer.

He sat on the edge of his bed and contemplated the box. Placing his index finger on the end of the box, he pushed it until the cover came completely off. He said aloud, "I want You to be with me! I want You to be with me always!"

The response was, *"I find you in my favor also."*

Chapter 6

*"For the Lord of all shows no partial-
ity, nor does he fear greatness, Because
he himself made the great as well as the
small, and he provides for all alike; but
for those in power a rigorous scrutiny
impends"* (*Wisdom* 6:7-8)

Tim planned on arriving at SIMI at 8:00 the next
morning but did not arrive until 9:50.

He stopped to help an old man whose garbage bag
ripped open, spilling all of the aluminum cans he had col-
lected. He helped the old man pick up the cans, and they
put them in the trunk of the Mercedes. He then took the
man and his cans to Woodlawn's Market for the recycling
money, then returned the man to his home. Tim might
not have noticed the old man's dilemma had not his
Companion commented on the oldster's plight.

Tim was not sure if he felt good about the time he
spent helping the man. He thought, "Surely I could have
contributed more to the world by doing what I do at my
company." His Companion made no comment, but Tim
felt His disapproval. With some reflection with his own
wisdom, he agreed that it was a worthwhile stop.

"Good morning, June."

"Good morning, Mr. Sorsen," said a surprised June.

"We didn't expect you back so soon."

"I'm afraid that doing nothing isn't for me."

"Well, Mr. Mills will be glad to see you. Today is the meeting with the Union and Employee Committee on the new contract. Mr. Martin said he was very uneasy without you."

"What time is the meeting"

"10:30."

"Any coffee?"

"Just made a fresh pot; I'll bring it in. Do you want me to tell Mr. Mills you'll be at that meeting?"

"Yes, please."

Tim sat with his coffee, trying to remember numbers and issues he had memorized for this meeting. He finished his coffee, reached into his desk, and found a leather-bound note pad. Passing June, he said, "Does Martin have all our files and materials for this meeting?"

"I'm sure he does, Sir."

Tim went into the conference room and was greeted by Martin who said, "Welcome back. That wasn't much of a vacation. I believe you know everyone here." Tim shook hands with Jim Smith and Carl Simpson, representing the union, and motioned and nodded to his four employees, the bargaining committee.

"Anyone wanting coffee, it's over in the corner, and there's ice water on the table," Martin said.

After some got coffee and some poured water, Jim Smith said, "I think we should address the salary issue here at SIMI first, for if we do not have an agreement on wages, we do not have any foundation for a new contract."

Tim replied, "I believe we have already proposed a generous four percent increase in salary."

Smith responded, "That is not acceptable. We are asking for a ten percent across the board increase to bring SIMI employees' salaries up to industry standards."

"Jim, our benefit package of salary, insurance, and retirement is above industry standard!"

"But we're not addressing insurance and retirement funds, Sorsen. We're talking about salary. Your employees cannot eat with insurance money. They cannot pay rent with retirement funds until they get them. For these employees to live in and about this community with any kind of lifestyle, they must have a ten percent increase. It's only fair to reward these employees for their efforts that have put SIMI in great financial shape, able to pay record dividends, and reinvest millions in its facility and equipment."

Jim continued on, but Tim's Companion got his attention with, *"He is right, you know. Making and having money is not wrong. But one must share what he has with others, specially with the deserving. You cannot deny their petition for just wages!"*

Tim was staring at the conference table as if in a trance. Everyone was staring at him, wondering what his response was going to be. Tim looked up and at Jim Smith saying, "If I were to agree to this ten percent across the board increase, what strings would be attached to this agreement?"

Tim's reply completely dumbfounded Smith. Never for a moment did he believe that he would be able to negotiate a ten percent salary increase with SIMI! He bowed his head, staring into his lap, trying to prepare himself for further argument, but there was nothing left to say. It was like he tried to lift a very heavy bucket only to find it empty!

"If you were to approve the contract with a ten percent salary increase, we would wave all other benefit demands and put the new contract to a membership vote within the week."

"I will sign the contract," said Tim standing to leave the meeting.

As Martin and Tim were walking from the meeting, Martin said, "I know you know, but I'm going to ask anyway. Do you know how much this increase is going to cost us?"

"I have a pretty good idea, but I'm sure you have the figures, so why don't you tell me?"

"It will be at least three quarters of a mil."

"You and I will have to look at smaller bonuses and sell more machines, Martin."

"I think you just assassinated SIMI. We won't be able to compete in the market," said Martin turning on his heels and leaving Tim standing in front of his office.

Walking into his office, Tim went over to the large wall mirror. Looking in at himself, he thought, "SIMI's Pit Bull, indeed. It's more like SIMI's John Wilkes Booth!"

His Companion queried, *"Why are you berating yourself? What you did was commendable. It was right and just!"*

"But You don't understand."

"I do not understand?!"

"Sorry, I have work to do."

"You?"

"We. June, will you come in, please."

June came in with her pad and a sheaf of papers as if she knew what he needed and sat in front of his desk.

"Would you tell us what we have to do today?"

She looked around the office and said, "Us?"

Tim snapped back, "What's on my agenda?"

June's face flushed, and she bent her head and started going through her note pad.

"I'm sorry, June, very sorry! I'm not myself today. . . . In fact, I haven't been myself since we received that damn Ark!"

She did not reply, but just looked at Tim knowing there was more to come.

"I cannot describe my feelings, or fathom my frustrations in my search for answers."

"Take some comfort, Sir, in that you're not the only one affected by the Ark. It has affected so many of us. Were you aware that Walters who first discovered the Ark has left our employment and his family and friends to become a Franciscan Brother?"

"Walters, a Brother?"

"Yes, Sir, and that's not all. Two other Receiving employees had to be terminated because they refused to work in that building. They said it was a holy place!"

Tim's Companion came in strongly with, *"This is very wrong! These men should not be punished for their show of respect, adoration, and above all for their beliefs!"*

June, see that these men are rehired with back pay and their benefits reinstated."

"Are you sure, Sir?"

"Very!"

"They were let go because we had no other openings."

"Have personnel work it out."

"Yes, Sir. Have you seen this morning's paper, or heard the news about that air controller, Franz Helms?"

"No, June. I usually listen to the news in the car, but I was interrupted this morning."

"I have a copy of the *News* at my desk."

"No, just tell me about it."

"Well, it seems Franz Helms and his family have disappeared! His neighbors say that the family have been gone for about two weeks. Franz told them that they were visiting the Holy Land."

"Israel?"

"Yes, Sir, but now Franz is gone too, not showing up for work. His neighbor and good friend said that Franz had said nothing of going anywhere. He suspects foul play."

"The *Washington Post* and CNN, however, claim that in the investigation of the missing plane, investigators believe the missing plane report by Franz Helms is a false report. The FAA and the State Department say their investigations are incomplete. The *Post* and CNN are sticking to their stories that the report was a false report. Both claim to have seen transcripts of the radar tracking from all the tracking stations. The plane was tracked to Greenland as an identified aircraft. It was tracked to the Azores as unidentified only because its crew did not identify when the craft flew over Greenland. According to the transcripts the same aircraft was tracked to the Azores and on to Israel's air space. This was confirmed by two other tracking stations.

"The big question is, why wasn't there an air scramble when an unidentified aircraft entered Israel's air space? This has got to be a first!"

"I'm impressed with your memory, June."

"If I hear or read anything that has to do with the Ark, I get a 'now-print.'"

"You say that the plane flew into Israel safely?"

"Yes, Sir."

"I don't know, June, if I'm pleased or displeased with this news. Why are we all so concerned about this Ark?"

"Have you seen the latest? All the stores are selling replicas of the Ark, from one to one hundred dollars."

"How sad!"

"Yes, it is."

"Well, I guess it's lunch time. Would you care to join me for lunch, June?"

She hesitated for a moment, then said, "I'd love to, Sir, but I already have a luncheon date with two of my old college chums. May I have a rain check?"

Tim, thankful that she did not actually say "no" with her gracious decline, said, "Of course. I'll be back around two or so."

"Yes, Sir."

His Companion asked, *"Do you often have lunch with your secretary?"*

"No. Sometimes when we're real busy, we'll send out for sandwiches and have a working lunch."

"What was the purpose of your lunch invitation today? It must have been pretty special."

Tim stared into the desk drawer he was about to close. He was suddenly very uncomfortable with his Companion's presence. He continued looking into the drawer while he thought about his motives for the invitation. After a few moments, with much difficulty, he thought, "I'm sorry." This gave him little relief. Closing the drawer, Tim stood up and said aloud, "I'm sorry, very sorry!" He turned and left the office.

Tim went downtown to "Turners." He liked their soups. As he was about to go into the restaurant, a tramp approached him and asked him for change to buy food. He ignored him and continued into the restaurant. The interior was very bright with broad, white-trimmed, lattice windows on two sides. The windows were bordered with dark red drapes and matching valances. The other two walls were stucco white, featuring large framed photos of floral gardens. The carpet was dark red. There were vases with three dark red roses on each white linen covered table, surrounded by white wooden chairs with dark red padded seats. The restaurant, crowded with diners, was very quiet. Only a few deadened sounds of the busy room reached the ear, which added to the relaxed atmosphere. He was seated immediately and was studying the menu when his Companion communicated with, *"You are going to eat while your brother goes hungry?"*

Tim continued looking at the menu without seeing. In thought, he replied, "I suppose I should have given him some money to buy something to eat."

"Real charity would be for you to share your meal with him."

"You mean in here?!"

"Do you find a difference between yourself and this man?"

"Well, for one thing, he's not dressed properly to come in here!"

"It is the only attire the man has!"

Tim rose to his feet as the waiter was about to take his order. He said, "Excuse me, I'll be right back; please hold my table."

He went outside and approached the man who was begging for food money.

"Would you like something to eat?"

"Yes, Sir!"

"Come with me."

"Where?"

"In here."

"I ain't going in there, just give me some money and I'll get my own grub."

"If you're really hungry, you'll come in and have a meal with me."

"The man stared at Tim, then challenged him by say-ing, "OK, Buddy, I'll go in there with you, but I bet they throw me out!"

Tim led him into the restaurant and to his table. Not as many people seemed to notice as he thought would.

They sat down at the table, and the beggar said, "You queer or a cop or somethin'?"

"No! What's your name?"

"Charlie."

"Mine's Tim. Here's a menu."

"Oh, I can't see none too good without my glasses. Why don't you order for me? I like meat."

"How hungry are you?"

"I haven't had anything to eat today. I had a good meal yesterday afternoon at the Soup Kitchen though."

The waiter came and asked, "Are you gentlemen ready to order?"

Charlie said, "Could I have something to drink?"

"Yes, of course, Sir. What would you like?"

"Bourbon."

"What brand, Sir?"

"Don't care, just bourbon."

"What would you like with that?"

"Don't want nothing with it! Just bourbon."

"And you, Sir?"

"A martini up, with 'Beefeaters' and an olive."

"Thank you. I'll return with your drinks and take your orders."

"You said you had a good meal yesterday at a soup kitchen. What is a soup kitchen?"

"It's a place where they give you free grub and don't hassle you or nothin'."

"Who runs it?"

"I don't know. They call it the Catholic Worker's Soup

Kitchen, but only some of them is Catholics. They're just a bunch of nice people who feed us."

There was an embarrassing silence while the two men waited for the waiter to return. Tim thought, "He is just like real people. What a stupid thought! He is real people! No, no, I mean like people I deal with every day. He does-n't use the greatest English, but my friends and associates are not all English majors." He looked at Charlie who was looking out the window and thought, "I like this guy."

Charlie was short and stocky, almost square. He was wearing a dark blue, pin-striped, business suitcoat, over a green plaid shirt, worn blue jeans and white running shoes. His face was tan with a rather large nose. He had brown hair that was starting to gray on the sides. "Cocky," was the descriptive word Tim was thinking. When this man, Charlie, answered a question, his blue-gray eyes would find Tim's as if adding, "So what?" to his answer.

The waiter returned with their drinks. He put Char-lie's bourbon in front of him and then went around the table to serve Tim. Charlie finished his drink in one gulp before Tim was served.

"May I have your orders, please?"

"Yes, please. I'll have a bowl of your chowder and a gar-den salad with roquefort dressing. My friend will have a bowl of your vegetable beef and a prime rib sandwich."

"Would you like a whole or half a sandwich?"

"Whole, and we'll have coffee later."

"Could I have another bourbon?"

"No, Charlie, we're here to eat, not drink!" Tim real-ized that he was tormenting Charlie every time he sipped his martini. He pushed it aside and said, "How long have you lived on the street?"

"Don't know—two or three years now."

"Do you like living on the street?"

"Buddy, livin' on the street is the worst thing in the world that can happen to a man. It's like the whole world belongs to other people and you're a fly, flying around. People keep shooing you away and making awful faces when they see you, like you was a piece of junk!"

"Are you going to stay on the street?"

"No Siree Bob. I'm going back to being an electrician, get a truck, and buy a home!"

"When are you going to do this, Charlie?"

"Soon as I get my head together and stop drinking—maybe soon."

"You're an electrician?"

"The best! Had my first class license. It still may be good; if it ain't, I can still pass the test again."

"Have any family?"

"Had a wife and three kids."

"Where are they?"

"Last I heard they were in Cedar Rapids, Iowa."

"What happened to make you leave your family? Was it your drinking?"

"Not really. I've always had this drinking problem, but I was sober for eight years after I got married. Things were great. We had three kids, a nice house, two cars, and two trucks. I really loved my wife and kids. Then my wife started shacking up with my neighbors and friends, and I fell off the wagon."

"Any chance of you getting back with your family?"

"No chance. She's already divorced me and her new old man has adopted the kids."

They finished their lunch after Charlie had a chocolate sundae.

Outside of the restaurant, Tim asked, "Can I give you a lift anywhere?"

"I ain't got nowhere to go."

Tim's Companion stirred his conscience with, *"We cannot leave this soul here with no place to go, shooing him away like the lowly fly!"*

"Where are you sleeping?"

"When I get a few dollars, I flop at the Lincoln Hotel on 53rd. Mostly I sleep in parks and in doorways."

"Come with me, Charlie."

"Where we going?"

"I'll take you over to the hotel and fix you up with a room."

"Why don't you just give me the money and I'll take care of it?"

"No way!"

They went to the parking garage and got Tim's car and drove to the Lincoln Hotel. The hotel was a pitiful, dirty place!

"What are your rates?"

"You can share a room for four bucks, or you can have your own room for ten."

"What do you mean share a room?"

"These rooms sleep four. So you got to share the room with three other guys."

"How much for a private room for a month?"

"Two hundred with a wash basin, toilet in the hall, and clean sheets once a week."

"He'll take a private room for a month," Tim said to the bathless desk clerk pointing toward Charlie.

He noticed that Charlie's last name was Evans when he signed the register and was given the key to number 417.

Tim took out one of his cards and gave it to Charlie saying, "When you're ready to stop drinking and go back to being an electrician, give me a call. I can help you."

As he started to leave, Charlie touched his shoulder, "Thanks for the grub an' this room," he said, holding up the key to 417.

Tim just smiled at his friend.

He arrived back at the waiting room to his office at 2:35. "Sorry I'm late, June, but I met a friend. Did I miss anything?"

"Yes, you did. Mr. Collins of Caterpillar was here but couldn't wait because he had to catch a plane to Peoria."

"The big boy himself, wow! Did he say what he wanted?"

"He said he'd give you a call."

Tim went into his office and worked on the stack of reports on his desk. When he had finished he looked at the time. It was 3:45.

His thoughts went back to Charlie. He wondered, "How would he get something to eat tonight? He said something about a soup kitchen. Makes one wonder why people do things like that." In Tim's mind it was as if his Companion cleared His throat to make His presence known. Tim immediately thought, "Of course, it's out of the goodness of their hearts, a goodness put there by God."

His Companion suggested, *"Maybe you should find out more about this good place."*

June came into the office saying, "Here's the afternoon mail, Sir."

"June, do you know anything about the Soup Kitchen?"

"Soup Kitchen? Do you mean like the ones that feed the very poor and homeless?"

"Yes."

"There are many such places run by organizations like the Salvation Army, churches, and just ordinary people helping people."

"The one I was thinking of is the Catholic Worker's Soup Kitchen."

"Oh yes, I know that one well. I go there quite often. Our church goes there once a month to serve meals, do dishes, scrub floors, or do whatever needs to be done."

"You say your church goes to the Catholic Worker's Soup Kitchen, but you're not Catholic?"

"Oh no, Sir, it's not like that. It's not a religious organization. The Soup Kitchen is a place where people who are socially concerned can help their fellowman. The only purpose of the kitchen is to feed the hungry. They do not preach or pray at the kitchen. They just try to create an atmosphere of a home, with a home cooked meal."

"Could I go down sometime?"

"Of course you can. Go down any weekday at 11:30 or 2:30. The people who go at 11:30 prepare the meal. The 2:30 people serve the meal, wash dishes, and clean the kitchen."

"I'd very much like to go."

"It's an experience you won't forget, Sir!"

"I'm all set here, June, if you'd like to leave. I have a few things on my desk to clean up, and then I'll be leaving."

"Will you be in tomorrow morning, Sir?"

"Yes."

He spent another forty-five minutes at his desk and called it a day.

Wally greeted Tim as he came into the kitchen from the garage: "Hello, how was your day?"

"Very interesting. What do we have here?" he said, looking at three very large sheet cakes that Wally was frosting.

"Oh, these are cakes that I baked for the Free Mission. They serve a free lunch to the street people. Every other week Sacred Heart of Jesus sends down fresh cake. I hope you don't mind?"

"Of course not, Wally. I think it's wonderful! Whatever gave you the idea of doing this?"

"I'm not real sure. All of a sudden I felt like doing something for someone else."

"I know the feeling well."

"You do?" Wally said, with some surprise in his voice. He then felt embarrassed and followed with, "I'm sorry, Sir. It's just that I thought you would hardly have time for such thoughts with your busy days."

"No, no, you're right! I haven't had time for such thoughts in my adult life, until lately when such thoughts and feelings have been brought to my attention. What's for dinner, Wally? Cake?"

"No, Sir, these cakes are promised! I was planning on chicken breast in a white wine sauce . . . if that's all right with you?"

"Super, Wally! I'm going to swim a few laps."

"Very good, Sir."

Tim went to his room and put on swim trunks and returned to his indoor pool. He flipped on the overhead lights. They flashed and went off. Tim grunted in disgust and flicked the switch on and off. Nothing happened. He went back through the kitchen, headed for the garage.

"Something wrong, Sir?"

"Yes, the lights won't stay on over the pool!"

"I know. You'll have to turn the pool heater off to turn the lights on, and then turn the heater back on. If you want to turn the heater off, I'll go out to the garage and reset the breaker."

"Thanks, Wally. Remind me to get the wiring fixed in this old house." He had gotten an estimate of $5,000 for higher amperage and new state-of-the-art wiring last year.

He went back to the pool, turned off the heater, waited a few moments, then turned on the overhead lights. They stayed on. He then went over and turned on the heater. The lights dimmed for a moment but stayed on.

Tim came to breakfast early next morning.

"Morning, Sir. What would you like for breakfast?"

"Morning, Wally. Do we have any Total?"

"Yes, Sir."

Wally poured a glass of orange juice and a cup of coffee and placed the morning paper in front of him. The headlines took Tim's attention away from either the coffee or the orange juice. They read, "**Israel Hides the Ark.**"

The story line was: "Israel again hides the Ark as did their ancestors, while people from around the globe clamor to see and receive news of the Ark."

The newspaper recapped the staging of the disappearance of the Israeli cargo plane, the fact that Israel let an unidentified aircraft enter their airspace without raising an eyebrow, and that they have not complained about the loss of the Ark. Israel's posture was now one of wanting the rest of the world to forget about the golden Ark.

"Read the news, Wally?"

"Yes, Sir."

"Doesn't look like this thing's going to leave us, does it?"

"That was what I was thinking this morning, Sir."

Tim and Wally ate in silence.

On the way to work, Tim thought about the Ark. He also thought about his Companion. He felt as if his communications with Him were a response to his new awareness of the Companion's presence, mentally reaching out and touching his Consort. Yet the more he pondered, the less clear was his understanding. He knew that the Ark did exist, but to his modern world programmed mind, having God with him as a constant Companion, did not compute.

His Companion joined his thoughts, *"With such reflections you will someday start having 'Ah Ha' waves. Continue these reflections and instead of 'Ah Ha,' you will be saying 'Amen'!"*

Tim parked his car in his carport at SIMI. He started walking briskly to the main office building when a strange feeling came over him. He became short of breath, and his arms and chest felt like pure lead; his chest had a burning pain. His Companion erupted in his senses with such force that He captured Tim's attention with, *"Stop, sit down on those steps!"* He sat down on the steps of the Tire Warehouse. Trying to breathe deeply, slowly his breathing became easier and the heaviness and pain subsided.

"You all right, Sir?" said an employee he didn't know.

"Oh yes, I just stopped to tie my shoe," he said bending over and faking shoe-tying. He arose and started slowly walking toward his office building. "What the hell was that?" he thought, now feeling fine.

His Companion, showing the concern and the sternness of a mother, blended with his thoughts, *"Tim, this was your body talking to you! This could be very serious! You must see your doctor right away!"*

June was at her desk, and Perry Ulrich was in a chair with a magazine on his lap.

"Good morning, June, and a big good morning to you, Perry. To what do I owe this honor?"

Perry, the purchasing director for the city and one of SIMI's best customers, responded, "Oh, I just have a couple of things I'd like to go over with you."

"Please, come in," Tim said pointing to his office door.

"There's fresh coffee on your desk, Sir."

"Thank you, June."

"Have a seat, Perry. Coffee?"

"Yes, thank you."

Tim poured coffee and asked, "How's the family, Perry?"

"They couldn't be better."

"How's Bill doing at Notre Dame?"

"Getting along by the skin of his teeth, but I think he'll stick it out. What I came to see you about is a little project I have going."

"Tell me about it."

"Well, I bought seventy acres out by Slough Creek. It's between Slough Creek and I-80."

"What are you going to do with land out there, Perry?"

"Well, let's say I got a tip that they're going to connect Shore Drive to I-80, and it'll go right through this property!"

"I don't know what you paid for the property, Perry, but it sounds like you stand to make some money on the deal."

"Yeah, and I think I can make the pot even sweeter."

"How so?"

"Well, the Feds and the State haven't released the news of the planned connection. So, before they make public their construction plans, I'm going to subdivide the land into lots, pour curbs and gutters for some streets, and dig a couple of basements. With the increased value I can show, I should be able to get my money back from my investment fivefold! You could help me by putting me in touch with some contractors I can trust."

Tim was silent, looking like he was in deep thought. He was hearing his Companion saying, *"This plan is fraudulent! You most certainly cannot help this man defraud and deceive the government and the tax payers of this community and of the nation!"*

He thought, "But this is one of my best customers. Besides, I'm not defrauding anyone!"

"Oh, but you would be taking part in the fraud if you help him!"

"Aren't you taking a big chance with 'conflict of interest,' Perry?"

"No, not really. I have this property in a family name on my wife's side. No one will be able to connect any transaction with me."

"Perry, I've been thinking hard, and I can't come up with anyone. Frankly, I wouldn't want to involve anyone's reputation in such a scheme."

"What do you mean, Tim?! If I hadn't bought that land, some other speculator would have."

"And subdivided it, Perry?"

"Such things are common practice. Hey, you've made a lot of slick business deals in your day, Tim Sorsen!"

"I'm sorry, Perry, I just can't think of anyone."

His Companion said, *"Be honest."*

Tim added, "I really don't want to recommend anyone, Perry."

Perry stood up, face flushed, and said, "I understand, Tim. I do expect you to keep what I've told you confidential! I have to leave now, I have a zillion things to do."

"Let's do lunch next week, Perry."

"Have your secretary call mine," said Ulrich as he went out of the office door.

Tim walked over to the mirror on his office wall and said to his image, "OK, Mr. Pit Bull, you just lost the city's business!"

His Companion countered, *"What you did was right!*

You should report this man to the authorities and separate yourself and your business from this person as far as possible!"

He grimaced and shouted within his mind, **"I just did!"**

Tim slumped in his chair, glowering at his desk.

June came in with the morning mail. Looking at Tim, she said, "You all right, Sir?"

"No, I'm not all right! I didn't feel well a half hour ago, and now I've made Ulrich mad, and I'm sure it'll cost us the city's business!"

"What happened, Mr. Sorsen?"

"Why don't you call Martin in here so you both will know what happened."

"Mary Lou, is Mr. Mills in?" . . . "Would you have him come into Mr. Sorsen's office, please?" . . . "Thank you."

"Good morning, Tim. Hi, June. What's up?"

"Martin, Perry Ulrich was just in here with a hair-brained scheme to screw the city, state, and federal government out of a bunch of money, and I insulted him!"

"What kind of a scheme?"

Tim described what Perry was up to.

Martin's response was, "You and I've seen worse schemes than that, Tim. You could have soft-pedaled around that."

"But I didn't soft-pedal; I told him the scheme stank and I didn't want any part of it!"

"I don't believe you, Tim! Something's going on with you that I don't understand."

"Wait. Before you go any further, let me tell you what I plan to do. I'm going to turn this over to the District Attorney."

"Tim, do you know what the hell you're doing? You're my boss, but you do this and you'll take this company down the tube! When this hits the papers nobody will touch SIMI with a ten foot pole! You said that you and I would have to look at smaller bonuses. Well, I think we're going to have to look at much smaller salaries!"

"Martin, I believe you're over-exaggerating. Why don't we talk about this over lunch?"

"Knowing what I know, I can't afford lunch," said Martin as he stomped out of Tim's office.

"I'm sorry Mr. Mills reacted so, Mr. Sorsen. It's just that he worked so hard getting the city's business."

"I'm sorry, too, June."

"Mr. Sorsen, is there any possibility that you could make amends with Mr. Ulrich?"

"No way, June! This guy is dead wrong! I'm not going to stand by what he's doing, and I'm not going to stand by and let him do it!"

"I admire what you're doing, Sir. It's the right thing to do! I know how hard this is for you."

"I have enough on my desk to keep me busy until lunch time, June. Also, I might have an extended lunch hour today—maybe 2:00 or 3:00."

"Fine, Sir."

Tim came into the lobby of the Lincoln Hotel. The smoke and urine smell was overpowering.

"Can you tell me if Charlie Evans is in?"

"How the hell would I know, Mister? Go up to his room and find out."

Sarcastically, Tim replied, "Thanks a lot!"

"Yeah, yeah, sure."

The door opened immediately when Tim knocked. Charlie and two other men were in the room. Visibility was down to about three feet due to the smoke in the room.

"Oh, hi Buddy," said Charlie, "Come on in and sit down."

He looked around the room and could tell that others were sleeping in the room besides Charlie.

Tim stood and said, "I was just in the neighborhood and thought maybe we could have lunch together."

"Sure could. Can I bring my buddies here?"

"Well, I kind of need to talk to you, Charlie."

"OK, guys, my buddy wants to talk to me; I'll see you later."

Charlie stood up and the others remained sitting. Charlie went out the door. Tim hesitated, wondering why the others didn't leave. He then followed Charlie out. He asked Charlie, "Is it OK to leave your friends in your room?"

"Oh yeah, they're sharin' the room with me."

"But I thought we got you a private room."

"Hey, you're not the only one who can be a nice guy. Those are my friends, and they don't have any place to sleep." They walked the rest of the way down the stairs in silence. After they got into the car, Charlie said, "My buddies and I are pooling our money for grub and stuff, and we're going to try to save enough for rent. That place sure does beat sleeping outdoors."

They parked the car in the parking garage and walked to Turners. They were seated, and the waiter approached, saying," May I get you gentlemen something from the bar?"

"Yes, please. I'll have a Beefeaters martini up with an olive, and my friend will have a bourbon up."

"No, no, I'm on the wagon!"

Tim looked at Charlie with surprise and said, "OK, cancel the drinks, please."

"No, you go ahead an' have your drink. It won't bother me none."

Tim nodded to the waiter.

"What caused you to go on the wagon, Charlie?"

"I don't know. Maybe you did—when we got talkin' about me being an electrician an' all. My buddies and I got a new rule: no drinking or you have to sleep outside."

"That's great, Charlie; glad to hear it! That's one of the reasons I wanted to talk to you today."

"You mean my drinking?"

"No, about your being an electrician. Why don't we order, and I'll tell you about it."

The waiter looked at Charlie, who was wearing glasses today and had been studying the menu. "I'll have a bowl of your asparagus soup, a Ruben, and black coffee."

"I'll just have a Ruben and black coffee.

"Charlie, I have a big old house, and it needs a new electrical service, a service with more circuits and higher amperage."

"Yeah, most older homes do. You would need wire and cables brought in from the pole transformer line, a new service box, and probably most of your house rewired."

"Exactly what I need."

"I would like to help you, but I couldn't do the job because I don't have no tools. I'm not sure my license is good in this state. Even so, I wouldn't take no shortcuts or do nothing illegal. When I work, I work by the book. You would have to get a city permit and all.

"I wouldn't want you to do anything illegal or take any shortcuts. I want it done right, city permit and all.

"Charlie, I run a large company. We would have all the tools you'd need. In fact, we have one truck that may be outfitted just right for you. If not, we would have the tools in tool supply. We would even have the wiring. All we would have to buy would be the service box and switches."

"I don't know what it would cost to reinstate or get a license in this state."

"Don't worry about it. You should make enough from the job to pay for it."

"You're going to pay me?"

"You bet. I would expect to pay you the going rate; I work by the book, too."

"Hey, Buddy, why are you doing this? I ain't never done nothin' for you."

"Well, it's like you say, Charlie, 'You're not the only one who can be a good guy.'"

Charlie had a pleased look on his face, almost a smile, and he shook his head in wonderment between bites of his sandwich and spoons of soup. "You know, I've been praying awfully hard lately for God to help me get off the street. God is good!"

"Yes, He is, Charlie."

Tim's Companion added, *"Amen."*

After lunch the two went back to the hotel to get Charlie's electrician's license and to see if his driver's license was current. They then went to the city offices and found out that Charlie could rewire Tim's house, but could not advertise for business in this state. They applied for a new state license using his out-of-state license to qualify. The fee of $625 was to come out of the proceeds from the rewiring job.

They then drove to SIMI and to the maintenance building. Tim took Charlie in to meet the maintenance chief. "Pete, this is Charlie Evans. Charlie, this is Pete Snyder, 'Mr. Fixit.'"

"Nice to meet you, Charlie."

"Nice to meet you, Buddy."

"Pete, Charlie is going to put in a new electrical service

and new wiring in my house. He's going to need tools and supplies. I was wondering if you could spare a van, maybe even the one with the electrical tools and supplies for a week or two?"

"I couldn't get along without that one, Sir! That unit is pretty much in demand every day. I could outfit that white 'Jimmy' in short order though."

"Anything wrong with the 'Jimmy'?"

"No, Sir, good running unit."

"He'll need you to help him with supplies. If he needs anything from the electrical supply houses, show him how to get them, and be sure that everything is marked 'T. Sorsen, personal.'"

"Charlie, I'll leave you with Pete. You can drive the 'Jimmy' to the hotel."

"No, Sir! I ain't leavin' no truck with tools parked in my neighborhood!"

"Never thought about that, Charlie. Why don't you come over to my office when you're ready, and I'll see you get back to the hotel. OK?"

Charlie nodded.

Tim sat down to a desk full of papers and a list of a dozen telephone calls. He picked up the phone and went about his tasks with a satisfied feeling.

Later on in the afternoon his Companion tugged at Tim's attention, *"Have you forgotten about Perry Ulrich and what he plans to do to the city, state, and federal government?"*

"I've tried not to think about it!"

"That is the easy way out, Tim, but we both know that it is not the right way."

Tim dialed the number of Jeff Pierce, an attorney retained by SIMI.

"Good afternoon, Tim. Who do you want to sue?"

"I don't want to sue anyone, Jeff. I just need some advice." He laid out the story of Perry Ulrich's devious plot in detail.

"My advice to you, Tim, is to forget about it. You know as well as I do that it would be very bad PR! That kind of publicity you and SIMI don't need. People are going to say that because you found the Ark you found religion."

"Number one, the Ark is not lost, and number two, maybe I did find religion. In any case, I'm going to expose Ulrich's venture."

"Don't you do anything, Tim! If you feel you have to do this, then let me do it for you. I know who to talk to and who not to tell. Maybe we can get by with a mere statement on what Perry confided to you. OK?"

"OK, Jeff, but don't spindle this on your desk. Get right on it."

"Hey, you'll be the first to know when the media starts pounding on your door! Gotta run, I hear a siren."

"Talk to you later, Jeff."

Chapter 7

> *"The people of Beth-shemesh were harvesting the wheat in the valley. When they looked up and spied the ark, they greeted it with rejoicing"* (*1 Samuel* 6:13).

The following Thursday Tim, who felt he had finished his work, was putting on his suit coat when June announced, "Mr. Evans is here."

"I'll be right out, June."

He joined June and Charlie in the outer office.

"Good night, June. I'm going to drop Charlie off at his hotel. See you tomorrow."

"Have a good night, you two."

On their way to the car Charlie reported, "Well, I think I have everything ready to do your house. It took longer than I thought, starting from scratch and all."

"I understand, Charlie."

"Mr. Snyder said I could keep my stuff and the truck over in Receiving. It's got bins big enough to hold the truck. He's going to get me a padlock to lock the bin. Trouble is, I don't know which building and which bin he's talking about."

"It's on our way out; I'll show you."

Tim drove into Receiving and to the receiving bins where they keep incoming shipments until they are complete. There were six large bins made of cyclone fencing. The bin doors were open except for two. Bin number six had a stenciled sign on it which said "EVANS." It also had an open padlock and key hanging on the door.

"There you go, Charlie. They have it all ready for you. Why don't you take the key with you, and then you can lock up your bin like this one," Tim said, glancing at the other bin and then doing a double-take. The other bin not only had a padlock, it had a cable lock and an electronic device with wires threaded through the chain link fencing. It was obviously an alarm system.

"What the hell is this?" He looked at the tag hanging on the door. It read, "PROPERTY OF THE UNITED STATES GOVERNMENT."

"Somthin' a matter, Buddy?"

"No, I just don't know what this could be."

"Looks like a big box under that tarp."

"Yes, it does, Charlie. I'll check on it in the morning."

Tim was having his dinner with Wally and sat stabbing his New York cut steak over and over again with his fork.

"That piece of meat is already dead, Sir. Is it tough?"

"No, it's fine, Wally. Sorry, I'm just bothered by something."

"Something to do with your business?"

"Yes and no. Let me bounce this off of you. We received an artifact in a motor box from Israel by mistake. There is a big mix-up as to who sent it. That gets straightened out. Then they ship it back to Israel, and they say the plane is lost. Israel claims it did not receive the shipment, but this squeaky door country is very quiet about not receiving the shipment. Today I'm in Receiving and find a bin made of chain link, locked and with some kind of a fancy alarm system wired to it. Inside there's a motor box like the one the Ark came in. There is a tag on the bin saying that it is the property of the US Government. Any thoughts, Wally?"

"I'm sure my thoughts are the same as yours, but that would be pretty bazaar! Do you usually know what they keep in those bins?"

"No, you're right, Wally. I shouldn't be jumping to conclusions. There could be a good reason for that locked bin."

Tim continued eating in silence, then suddenly dropped his fork with a clatter on the table, pushed back his chair, put his arm over the chair back, and crossed his legs. He lifted his other arm from the table and pointed his finger at Wally saying, "We never put an alarm system on a bin. We don't own any such alarm systems!"

"Is there anybody you could call now that could tell you what's in that bin? I know you, Sir. You won't rest until you find out what's in that bin."

"Yes, I think I'll give Martin a call . . . or maybe Guy." Tim sat there in the same position, thinking.

Wally said, "Why don't you finish your meal before you call, Sir. It would be a shame to waste it after you killed it."

Tim pulled himself back up to the table, smiling at Wally's humor.

Martin answered the phone, "Good evening, the Mills' residence."

"Martin, I was in Receiving this afternoon, and one of the holding bins is locked up and has some kind of alarm system on it. Do you know what's in it?"

"Beats me, Tim. You ask Guy?"

"No, he wasn't around. I just thought that it was strange to have one of the holding bins wired with an alarm."

"Hey, Receiving is becoming a real strange and spooky place, Tim."

"There's a tag on the bin—not one of our tags—which says, 'Property of the US Government.'"

"Oh yea, yea, I know what that is. That's a bunch of stuff the . . . oh . . . you know . . . the Secret Service left here. It's some of their surveillance equipment—you know, like cameras, motion detectors, and other outer-space junk. But I thought they were only going to leave it here a couple of days. Why don't you give Guy a call. He should know more about it. You just think I'm the smartest man in the world, Tim. I'm really not."

"If you were, the world would be in pretty poor shape! Good night, Martin."

"'Night, Tim."

Guy's wife Irene answered the phone, "Hello."

"Hello, Irene, this is Tim Sorsen. How are you?"

"Just fine, Mr. Sorsen. How are you?"

"Just fine, Irene. Is Guy there?"

Irene did not answer Tim, but he heard her call to Guy, "Telephone, Guy. It's Mr. Sorsen!"

After a short pause, Guy answered, "Hello."

"Hello, Guy, sorry to disturb your evening, but I have a question for you."

"You aren't disturbing me; I wasn't doing nothin' except watchin' TV."

"Guy, holding bin number five is double locked and has an alarm system on it. Can you tell me what's in the bin?"

"Yes, Sir. It's a motor box full of electronic equipment which belongs to the government. Those locks on the alarm system ain't ours. They belong to the government, too. Mr. Ryan in security takes care of the alarm. It's all on the up and up, Sir. We're chargin' them for the space, like we do all customers."

"Do you have an inventory of what's in the box?"

"Not a regular inventory, like we keep when we use the storage for our regular customers. All our inventory sheet says is 'Electronic Equipment.'"

"Did you help them pack the 'Electronic Equipment' in the motor box, or did any other SIMI employee help?"

"No, Sir. They musta packed it the day they packed the Ark. They made all of us leave the building. Have I done something wrong, Sir?"

"No, no, no, Guy. I was just curious about that bin with all its locks and the alarm system. You have satisfied my curiosity, Guy. What are you watching on TV?"

"The fights on Channel 41."

"Well, I'll let you get back to your fights. Thanks for your help, Guy."

"Anytime, Mr. Sorsen."

Tim took an apricot brandy into the den and sat in his recliner. He wanted to collect his thoughts about this turn of events. Before he had time to relax and sip his brandy, his Companion interrupted his intended relaxation with, *"Your government and Israel are deceiving the world! They are duping all the peoples of the world who are interested in the Ark's true whereabouts. I am not arguing the value or importance of the Ark. I am saying that all of their lies and deceitful actions concerning the Ark should be exposed to all!"*

"I haven't deceived anyone about the Ark!"

"If you do not speak up about your suspicions, then you will be part of their lies!"

"What if the Ark isn't in that motor box? You know what's in that box. Why don't You tell me?"

"You forget, I am within your mentality and use your knowledge."

"I already have to face the media and perhaps be summoned by a Grand Jury over trying to expose Ulrich's scheme. What kind of furor will this create, if I say that the Ark is still here at SIMI in the Receiving building?"

"You have no other choice! We both know Truth is the only path. To use a phrase you use, 'no pain, no gain.'"

"What the hell would I gain by exposing my government's deception?"

"Let's say you might not gain Hell!"

"You know what all this is going to do to SIMI!"

"You know what is right and what is wrong, Tim. You have the freedom to choose either."

The following morning, Tim was walking from his carport when he noticed a group of people in front of his office building. "Oh no, it's the media," he thought!

"Mr. Sorsen, did Perry Ulrich offer you money to help him?"

"How come SIMI has had so many contracts with the city, Sir?"

The other questions were lost among the other questions.

Tim made his way through the door blocked to others by Chet Ryan. Tim said, "Thanks, Chet." Chet nodded. Entering the waiting room to his office he said, "Good morning, June . . . I think?"

"Good morning, Sir. Sorry about the big greeting outside. We tried to warn you at home, but you had already left for work."

"It's all right, June. I've been expecting such a greeting. Can you get me Jeff Pierce on the phone, please?"

"He's here, Sir, in your office."

Tim looked surprised, but made no comment and went into his office.

Jeff was sitting in front of Tim's desk, where he had his open briefcase sitting, working on some papers. He was a big man with a full head of black hair, black eyes under heavy black eyebrows, with a black moustache. He was wearing light gray slacks, black shoes, light blue sport shirt, under a dark gray sport coat. The sport shirt was open at the neck, displaying a thick gold chain and more black hair. The backs of his large hands holding the papers he was working on were also covered with the dark hair. Jeff was known as a swinger on the social set. "Good morning, Jeff, good timing."

"Good morning, Tim. I planned it this way. I released the story early this morning to three networks and two newspapers so it would hit the six o'clock news and tomorrow's papers. That way it gets less concentrated exposure."

"Where do we go from here, Jeff?"

"Well, first we have a cup of coffee, relax a few, then go down and talk to them."

Jeff poured two cups of coffee from Tim's thermo and sat down in front of the desk, motioning to Tim to sit in his chair.

"Is this thing going to get real sticky, Jeff?"

"Well, it didn't cause as much commotion this morning as I thought it was going to, but you're right—it could get messy. I'm sorry to say that the American public seems to have some kind of code that says whistle-blowing is not right, even if the whistle-blower catches the culprit red-handed."

"Oh great, then I'm really in deep trouble!"

"Not necessarily so, Tim. This is not the mayor. This is an underling in the city government. Don't make a federal case out of it!"

"Jeff Pierce, I wish you hadn't said that!"

Not knowing the significance of Tim's answer, Jeff said, "Let's take one problem at a time and go down and talk to them. And, Tim, let me do all the talking, **please!**"

Jeff spoke to the news media saying, "Good morning, ladies and gentlemen. As you know, I released the story that there is a plot by a city government employee to defraud the city and state out of a considerable amount of money! We are unable to make any further disclosures at this time. The reason for this would be because our allegations could bring an investigation, or be passed on to a Grand Jury or other legal action. So to protect the rights of this city government employee, we must decline to answer your questions."

"Mr. Sorsen, wasn't Perry Ulrich one of your best friends?"

"Yes, Perry is a goo. . . ."

"Jeff **boomed** in with, "Tim, please, I would advise you not to answer any questions about Mr. Ulrich at this time!"

"Mr. Sorsen, is this a possible ploy for more publicity for your company, since the Ark is lost and not in the news as much?"

"The Ark is not lost! It is here at SIMI in the Receiving building!"

For what seemed like frozen time, the silence was deafening! Jeff, who was about to speak, still had his mouth open, one arm in the air as in a gesture, looking at Tim in disbelief!

Also disbelieving was the newsman who had asked the question. He repeated Tim's statement back to him being very precise, without expression in the form of a question: "The Ark is not lost. It is here at SIMI in the Receiving building?"

"Yes."

Three newsmen were racing toward the parking lot to their cars where they possibly had communication equipment.

A newswoman asked, "How can that be? The Ark was flown out of here on an Air Force helicopter to O'Hare Field."

"It never left here it was a decep…."

"**Tim, Tim,** that's all for now!" Jeff was pushing Tim back through the office door while speaking over his shoulder, "Thank you for coming. We'll have more on this later."

On their way back to Tim's office, Jeff was screaming at Tim, "Man, did you know you were on TV and radio? Where the hell did you get this story? How can I be your attorney when I'm not filled in as to what's going on?!"

Tim was saying, "Sorry, sorry," but too softly to be heard.

People were looking out of their office doors at all the commotion. Back in Tim's office, Jeff poured himself a cup of coffee, sat down in a chair, placing his coffee on Tim's desk. "Now, Tim, please tell me what this is about–the Ark being here at SIMI in the Receiving building." Tim related the story and particulars about bin number five and how he made his deductions that the Ark never left SIMI.

"A strong case of circumstantial evidence, I admit, Tim, but not proof beyond the shadow of a doubt. Not proof enough to stick your neck out like you did! Even if the Ark is in that bin, why do you want to meddle in the government's business? Evidently this is some kind of action on the part of the Feds to ease a stressful situation. We know that they felt that the Ark would make a good terrorist target for Israel's enemies."

June broke in, "Excuse me, Mr. Sorsen, NBC is on line one."

Jeff yelled from his position across the desk, loud enough for June to hear, "Tell them Mr. Sorsen is out!"

Tim's Companion reacted with, *"That would be a deliberate lie!"*

Tim responded with, "Tell NBC that I'm not accepting any calls—that I'm in conference. That will apply to all media calls, June."

His Companion came in with, *"I will give you that one,"* which made Tim smile.

"Yes, Sir," June replied.

Back to their conversation, Jeff said, "Tim we can probably repair the damage done by claiming it's a misunderstanding. Tell them that you meant the Ark is here at SIMI in spirit."

Tim's other self queried, *"You wouldn't consider this, would you?"*

"No, Jeff. I feel what the two governments are doing is wrong. This news of the Ark belongs to the people of the world. If our country is allowed to manipulate the news by falsifying events, then we are in deep trouble."

"Tim, I don't know what's come over you. However, you do pay my fee, so please keep me informed as to what's going on and what you want me to do, and I'll try my best to produce."

"Thanks, Jeff. I understand how you feel and the tough situation I'm putting you in."

"Why don't you get in touch with your security and see if they can keep more people out of SIMI than they did last time."

"You really think that's going to happen again?"

"You bet I do! It will be different this time, too. This time they'll be mad! Nobody likes to be duped, especially by their own government. You talk to your security people, and I'll call Chief Johnson for help in the streets outside. Let's get the jump on this thing before it happens."

Chet Ryan said, "Yes, Sir, Mr. Sorsen. We'll get ready. I won't let that happen again. We'll close all the gates and the bay doors to Shipping and Receiving. No one gets in unless they're supposed to! I'll call in extra people."

"Thanks, Chet. Keep me posted."

Jeff contacted Chief Johnson, who agreed with the precaution, and would close off the streets around SIMI. He would also send a unit of armed guards to protect the Ark.

Jeff then contacted Chet advising him to admit the contingent of police to guard the Ark.

Jeff came back to Tim's office. "So far so good. Maybe with a little luck, we'll come out of this no worse for the wear. Tim, for the time being I think it best that I stick pretty close to you. Two heads are better than one. For today at least, I'll be your constant companion."

"**Oh boy**, just what I need!"

"Sorry, Tim, but I think it'll help us stay out of trouble."

Tim did not reply for he knew Jeff did not understand his dilemma.

June interrupted, "Secretary William Bates is on the phone."

"Put him on the squawk box," Jeff instructed.

"Hello, Bill. You find that order for the earth movers?"

"No way, Tim. I'm trying to find out what the hell is going on at SIMI now?"

"I think the shoe is on the other foot. Why don't you tell me what's going on here at SIMI?"

"Explain."

"Well, you could start by telling me what you have stored here in bin number five?"

"As far as I know, we don't have anything stored at SIMI. Tim, why don't you back up and fill me in?"

Tim related the details about the mysterious box in bin number five.

"Tim, this would make a bad 'B' movie. No one would believe the story! OK, let's start with the State Department; we have nothing stored at SIMI. I cannot speak for the other government agencies involved, but you can bet I'll know within the hour! Tim, my staff and I will get on this right away. I should have an answer for you in an hour or so. If what I think is true, you'll be able to take an ax and sledge and find out what's in your surprise package. By the way, am I on the squawk box?"

"Yes, Bill. I have Jeff Pierce, company attorney, here with me."

"Hello, Jeff. I better review what I've said. Tim, I think you are becoming paranoid. Stick by the phone, I'll be back." Dial tone.

Jeff scooted back in his chair, crossing his legs saying, "I wouldn't miss this even if I lose a ton of business today!"

Tim and Jeff, while waiting for Bates, kept abreast of the happenings by looking out of the office windows and checking with Chet Ryan. Yes, the people and cars were coming already, but they were being stopped by the police and barricades. There was a small crowd around the front gate. They assumed that this was the media. There appeared to be no one in SIMI except employees. They waited, paced, and Tim tried to work with some papers on his desk. He kept looking at his wristwatch, even though he had a large digital desk clock directly in front of him.

At 12:30 p.m., they still had not heard from Bates and decided to have lunch at SIMI's lunchette. They took a cellular phone and proceeded to the lunchette. Jeff ordered cherry pie à la mode with coffee. Tim had a ham and cheese sandwich and coffee. The employees who were there kept looking at them because Tim very seldom ate there. They returned to the office and waited until 2:34 p.m. before Secretary Bates called.

"Tim, I was partly right this morning. The United States Government, including all of its agencies, have nothing stored at SIMI! However, hold up on that sledge hammer. The Secret Service would like to witness the opening of that crate. They have someone coming over from the local federal offices there on Simms Street. I would imagine that they will be there shortly as they were contacted by Washington over half an hour ago."

"OK, coach, I got the ball; now what do I do?"

"I don't know about you, Tim, but I'm damn curious about what's in that box!"

"I am, too, but you people have been handling this thing."

"No longer. Use whatever company procedure you use in a case like this."

"We've never had a case like this!"

"You got one now. Maybe the Secret Service will have some guidelines for you."

"Do you want me to call you after we open it?"

"No, Tim. The Service's second call after they determine what's in the crate will be to me. Talk to you later . . . and, Tim, aren't you getting tired of seeing your name in the paper?"

"Very funny, Bill. Thanks for your help."

Tim had June contact Chet at the front gate to have him send the Secret Service over to Receiving. He cleaned up a few last papers on his desk, then with Jeff went to Receiving.

Tim was showing Jeff bin number five when he noticed Charlie had the white "Jimmy" backed into bin number six and was loading supplies.

"Hello, Charlie."

"Hi, Buddy. Whatcha' doin' down here?"

"Oh, I never did find out what was in this bin, so today we're going to find out. By the way, I was hoping I would find you around today. I have a check for you—a deposit on the house wiring. It's certified so you won't have any trouble cashing it."

Charlie took the check and looked at it. "I remember when a thousand dollar check didn't look very big to me. Right now it sure looks big! Thank you."

Tim introduced Charlie to Jeff, telling him how Charlie was starting up an electric contracting business and would need to incorporate. Jeff gave Charlie one of his business cards.

Tim left the two talking and went looking for Guy. He found Guy talking to two Secret Service men who were looking for Tim. Tim briefed everyone on the opening. He asked the agents if it was all right to break into bin number five. They advised him that they were just there to observe.

They all returned to the bin. Guy looked at the locks and said, "Why don't we get Pete Snyder over here to get these locks off?"

Tim asked, "What about the alarm?"

"I thought that Mr. Ryan was taking care of it, but he told me he didn't know anything about it."

"Hey, Charlie, come take a look at this alarm. Where do the wires go? If it's set off, who will know?"

He came over and started inspecting the alarm system. After a few moments, he said, "These wires don't go nowhere. The alarm uses the wires like the spider does to detect motion or breakage. The alarm is a silent radio alarm. If this alarm is tripped, it sends somebody a signal."

"A signal to whom?"

"I don't know, Buddy. Why don't we trip it and find out who answers?"

"Great idea!" responded one of the Secret Service agents. "Let me contact Chief Johnson before you trip the alarm."

A SIMI maintenance truck pulled in and backed up to the locked bin. Pete Snyder jumped out saying, "Guy, I thought I'd save some time and just cut those locks with an acetylene torch."

"So, OK with me," said Guy, looking at Tim for approval.

Tim responded to the building excitement, "Slow down. Let's wait for the Secret Service to notify the police what we're doing. Get your equipment ready."

Guy and Pete pulled the torch from the truck to see if the hoses were long enough. They seemed fine, so they laid the torch in front of the door.

Guy asked, "What should we do first, cut the locks or trip the alarm?"

Charlie quickly came back with, "Won't make no difference. If you cut them locks it will trip the alarm."

The Service agent was back and conferring with Tim who said, "It's a go." A loud **"pop"** was heard, practically at the same time "go" was heard, when Pete ignited the torch and pulled down his mask and adjusted the torch's flame. Flame and sparks flew as Pete cut through the locks–a dramatic and exciting scene–with all wondering when Mr. Spider would appear and who he might be!

When the last lock fell off, Charlie went up and put his ear to the alarm, "I can't tell if this alarm went off or not, but I'll bet someone besides us knows somebody's in this bin!"

Guy and the other Receiving Department employees went to work on the crate. It was opened faster than any other shipping container had ever been opened at SIMI. Nails screamed, sides dropped, styrofoam was tossed aside.

Sitting there in the middle of all the debris was the Ark of the Covenant!

Chapter 8

"You say, 'The LORD's way is not fair!'
Hear now, house of Israel: Is it my way
that is unfair, or rather, are not your
ways unfair?" (*Ezekiel* 18:25).

Tim arrived at work at 7:29 next morning. He left home even before Wally was awake. No one had come into the office as yet, although he thought he saw someone in Accounting when he went by.

He went into his office, and his eyes were drawn to a white business envelope on his desk. He couldn't help noticing. It was the only thing there. It was standing up against his pen holder in the center of his very clean desk. Now Tim knew he could predict nothing, yet he knew that this envelope did not contain good news!

> Mr. Tim Sorsen, President
> Sorsen's International Machine Inc.
>
> Dear Sir:
>   I would like to submit my resignation as Vice President of SIMI as of this coming October 31.
>   It saddens me to leave you and the dear

employees of this fine company. I feel, however, that due to the direction the company is going of late, I can further my career and benefit my family better elsewhere. You, Tim, and SIMI have been a big part of my life. I thank you and the company for all the great benefits given me!

Respectively yours,
Martin Mills

Tim read and reread Martin's letter. "What the hell can happen next? I'm probably going to be called up by the Grand Jury to testify against one of SIMI's best customers, on whom I informed. I informed on another very big customer, Israel. I granted a contract to our employees that will raise our cost so high we won't be able to compete in the market! Now as my ship is sinking, my good friend and long-time associate is leaving me!"

A startled June said, "You're early, Mr. Sorsen."

"Good morning, June, It's a sorry morning."

"Did you have a problem with those people like I did?"

"It wasn't too bad when I came in."

"Did you hear that someone was shot last night trying to drive his pickup through the fence on the south side of Receiving?"

"Oh God, no, June, this can't be happening!"

"The driver is OK with only a superficial wound."

"Thank God!"

His Companion came on strong, *I am offended by your thanks! You are only showing relief for your lighter burden. Your concern was not for the driver of the car.*

Tim knew this to be true, which made him feel even worse.

The phone rang and June apologized, "Sorry, Sir, I

The phone rang and June apologized, "Sorry, Sir, I switched the phone to your office. I didn't know you were in here." She answered the phone, "T. Sorsen's office. . . . Just one moment, please. . . ." Nodding toward the receiver, she said to Tim, "This is Officer Romero. He's in Sales downstairs and would like to come up to talk to you about some late developments concerning the Ark."

"Have him come up."

"Sir, Mr. Sorsen will be expecting you."

"Read this, June," Tim said, handing her Martin's letter of resignation. He waited for her to read it.

"This is awful, Sir, simply awful! I don't understand what's going on here at SIMI. It's almost like someone's cast a spell over this company!"

"All we can do is carry on, June. See if Romero's in your office yet."

He sat at his desk and reached for his thermo. It was empty, of course. June just arrived at work.

"Officer Romero is here."

"Please send him in."

"May I bring coffee?"

"Oh, yes."

Romero came into the office, "Good morning, Mr. Sorsen."

"Good morning, Lieutenant. Please have a chair."

June discreetly filled Tim's thermo.

"I thought you might be interested in our latest findings on who may have placed the alarm on your receiving bin."

"You bet I would! Coffee?"

"No, thank you, Sir, but you please go ahead."

"Thanks, I need a cup. Tell me what you've found."

"Well, you remember that the alarm was actually a small transmitter that detected motion or open circuits.

One of our officers suggested we should look around the neighborhood for a receiving antenna of the same size as the one on the alarm. Seems this officer is a ham radio operator, and he said that receiving and transmitting antennas are cut to the same size and frequency. He also said that we shouldn't have to look far because the transmitter was of very small wattage.

"We didn't have to look far. We found such an antenna in an apartment window right across the street. So we got an SW and went in."

"What is an SW?"

"Search warrant. The apartment had no occupants, but we did find a receiver for the alarm. We also found a letter in a briefcase from the US Army, with an open date, to SIMI, releasing the crate to the bearer.

"Now I know this sounds like 'Mission Impossible,' but there's more! Behind the apartment, in a garage, we found a US Army one-ton truck with a canvas top. We checked the truck out and found it was a stolen truck, repainted olive drab with Army identification."

"Hey, nothing surprises me anymore! What do we do now?"

"Well, Sir, I'm telling you this because we'd like to tighten up security. It all seems very clandestine, and we don't know what to expect next."

"Of course, do whatever you deem necessary. Please work with our Mr. Chet Ryan."

"Of course, Sir. He's a good man. We'll also keep you advised as to any happening."

"Thank you for this latest information."

"A good day to you, Sir."

After Romero left, Tim asked June to bring his agenda and anything that needed his attention.

"Yes, Sir, I'll be there in just a moment." This was an

unusual response for June, who always responded immediately to his beck and call. His coffee had cooled enough
for drinking, so he sipped his coffee and drummed his
fingers on his desk, keeping his mind blank, for he didn't
want to think.

June came into his office; she wasn't carrying her pad
or any papers. Her face was colorless, and her expression
was one of showing tremendous effort not to show emo-
tion. She sat down in a chair directly in front of Tim's
desk. She looked directly at him but said nothing, then
looked down.

He said, "What's wrong, June?" in the most soothing
voice he could muster, for he sensed that she was having
great difficulty with what she was about to say.

She again looked at Tim and said, "Mr. Sorsen," she bit
her lower lip. "Mr. Sorsen, Charlie Evans is dead!"

He wanted to stand up and shout, but he sat and softly
said, "Are you sure, June?"

"Yes, Sir."

They both sat in silence for a moment, then Tim
asked, "How?"

"They say he was beaten to death for some money."

At this, Tim **did** jump up and shout, "My God, I just
gave Charlie a thousand dollars yesterday!"

Oh no, Sir! I feel so sorry for you! I know how you
liked Charlie!"

"June, have Jeff Pierce follow up on this. If Charlie has
no family, I want him to have a decent burial and
funeral."

"Yes, Sir."

Tim turned and faced the window; he didn't want June
to see his face. He was fighting hard to control his emo-
tions. With some effort to control his voice, he said, "I'm

going to take the rest of the day off. I know things are in a turmoil around here, but there's something I must do. It might even help the situation here. Thanks, June, for your sensitivity."

She did not respond, only closed the door softly behind her.

Tim went to his car and drove home. It was not a conscious effort for he was unaware of the crowds around SIMI and the drive home.

He entered the house and went directly to his bedroom and the night stand. He opened the drawer and reached into the drawer with both hands, picking up half of the match box with each hand–the bottom in one hand and the sliding top with the other. He quickly assembled and closed the match box. Holding it tightly closed, he went down to the den. From the drawer of the desk he took out the tape dispenser, tore off two small pieces of tape and sealed both ends of the box.

Tim turned and went back to his bedroom, put the match box in the drawer of his night stand, and closed it. He laid on his bed, burying his face in his pillow, and wept in sadness and in frustration. He thought, "God is not fair! Why doesn't He use our rules? Why doesn't He see things like we do? Why doesn't He do what He ought to do?"

Chapter 9

"For he wounds, but he binds up; he smites, but his hands give healing" (*Job* 5:18).

Tim arrived at SIMI at 8:00 a.m. sharp. He did four hours of paperwork in one hour. He left word with Mary Lou that he wanted to see Martin as soon as he came in. June announced, "Mr. Mills is here to see you." This was unusual, for Martin always checked with June to see if there was anybody with him. If not, he would walk in. "Send him in, please."

"Good morning, Martin."

"Good morning, Tim."

"Let's get right to it, Martin," said Tim placing the white business envelope containing Martin's resignation between them.

"We both know that I've been acting strange, but let me tell you, you also have been acting strange. In the past if you didn't agree with me or my actions, you'd argue until we agreed. I've seen the time when you'd argue all day long and then call me up at home and argue more. Sometimes we'd compromise; sometimes one of us would see the other's wisdom.

"About you being able to better yourself elsewhere, that's a bunch of **bull roar**! SIMI has been very good to you and your family. Financially, your family should never want!

"As far as the future is concerned, you can't duplicate what you have here. I'm sixty-two; you're fifty-one years old. I'll step down as president very shortly, and you're number one in line! As you know, my wife, my son, and my daughter were killed in the same accident. There is no member of my family who is interested or qualified in the management of SIMI.

"When I said I'd step down shortly, I meant that I'll step down as soon as I straighten out the recent messes I've made.

"OK, how am I going to do this? To start with, there's not a lot I can do about Perry Ulrich. It's passed the point of no return. I doubt the city can exclude us from bidding on any machinery purchases made by the city. While Perry might not like what I did, there are many others who think I did the right thing. I would appreciate anything that you can do about this. I'm sure you'll get to know whoever replaces Perry and you'll be able to cultivate a relationship.

"As far as Israel's concerned, we'll cooperate with them in every way we can to cover their embarrassment and ours.

"To counteract the new wage contract I granted, we'll trim our work force to the point that we'll maintain our present payroll. If we grant only cost of living increases for the next three years, it'll balance out. We both know we have a lot of people hiding out in small offices, a lot of chiefs compared to the number of Indians we have, and a lot of places where we have two men doing one man's work."

Tim stopped, looking directly at Martin. Martin said nothing, looked down for a moment, and then stood up, reached across the desk, picked up the envelope. He walked around the desk motioning for Tim to stand up. The two men embraced awkwardly. On his way out, Martin said over his shoulder, "Now that you're back in form, I'll have Mary Lou bring you some dog biscuits. I'll keep you posted on the city thing."

Tim picked up the phone and dialed the city police department to find out about Charlie Evans. He knew he had asked Jeff Pierce to take care of it, but he wanted to know firsthand that Charlie's death and funeral were treated with respect. After much switching from one person to another, he finally got Officer Romero. The lieutenant told him he knew of the case, but that it was not his. He transferred the call to a Detective Eugene Brown.

"Detective Brown. How may I help you?"

"Detective, this is Tim Sorsen. I'm a friend of the late Charlie Evans."

"Timothy R. Sorsen, President of Sorsen's International Machine Inc.?"

"Yes."

"You're on the top of my list of people I have to contact today. What can I do for you?"

"I would like to know if Charlie had any family and how the funeral's being handled."

No family so far; we're treating him as a transient. His funeral will be handled by the state."

Tim responded, "If no family claims the body, I will be responsible for the arrangements, funeral, and all expenses."

"That's sure mighty nice of you, Sorsen. One of the things I wanted to talk to you about is what your connection with Charlie Evans is."

"I met Charlie panhandling on the street. Found out he was an electrician and was trying to help Charlie get back on his feet by hiring him to rewire my house with state-of-the-art wiring."

"You ever pay him any money?"

"Yes, I just gave him a check for a $1,000 as part payment for the wiring."

"OK. That solves part of the mystery of where he got the money. We found a deposit slip from First Bank for $940."

"You mean they killed Charlie for $60?!"

"Hey, $60 is a lot of money in Charlie's world! Why would you want to hire a guy like Charlie without an electrician's license? Were you trying to save a buck?"

"You haven't done your work very well, Detective. Charlie does have a license. We took care of that, and if you'll check, you'll find we also had a permit. He was supposed to start yesterday; he has all the supplies stored in a bin in our Receiving building along with an old van of ours he was going to use to transport tools and supplies."

"Hey, these are all questions I was going to ask you. You sure are making my job easier. As a matter of routine and a reason for my boss to give me a paycheck, could I come out and see this equipment of Charlie's?"

"Of course. Come to Receiving and tell them you'd like to see bin number six. I'll tell them you're coming."

"Thank you for all this information, Mr. Sorsen. I don't believe I'll need to see you unless something comes up.

"Pertaining to getting Evans' body, have your mortician contact the city morgue; I'll have it all cleared for you. Remember he has $940 in the bank. Your mortician will know how to handle this as his estate."

"Thank you for your help."

"Thank you, Sorsen."

Tim immediately dialed Jeff Pierce. Jeff was out, and he left detailed instructions for Jeff to handle arrangements for Charlie's funeral.

Tim then spent the better part of four hours in conversation with people in the Israeli government. It seems that Israel felt they had some egg on their face. This resulted in them offering to put the Ark on public display in seven major US cities. The announcement would reveal that this arrangement was suggested by the management of SIMI. The admission that would be charged would cover the monumental security cost.

Tim also offered the Receiving building of SIMI to prepare the Ark for showing.

Tim then made an appointment with his personnel director to research possible ways in which to cut SIMI's payroll.

The following evening Tim walked into Simms Funeral Home and was greeted by a pleasant young man in a dark suit. "May I help you, Sir?"

Tim was confused, and thought, "Should I say that I want to see Charlie Evans' body, or that I want to see Charlie Evans?" He said, "I'm a friend of Charlie Evans."

"Yes, Sir, right down this hall and through the door on the end. Would you like to sign the book?"

Tim was the third person to sign. One person from Peoria, Illinois, and the other didn't put an address.

"Excuse me, Sir. I noticed you're Tim Sorsen."

Tim nodded.

The young man extended his hand and said, "I'm Jefferson Simms, Jr. Excuse my detective work, but I noticed your name when I put the book back.

"We didn't know Mr. Evans and didn't have any photos of him, so if we don't have him looking natural, please let us know. We did have problems with his bruises and abrasions. If we can be of any other assistance to you, let us know."

Tim entered the rectangular room at the middle of one narrow end. The room had straight-back, padded chairs, four on each side of the center aisle. There were four rows of these chairs which filled about half of the room. The other sides of the room had an over-stuffed couch and chair along the walls. The casket was on the other narrow end of the room as if on center stage.

Tim walked to the casket past two other men seated one on each side.

Charlie did look a little strange, and Tim could tell his face was a little distorted. Tim inspected his face carefully, and Charlie looked like Charlie. Tim felt a warmness come over him. Why did he feel this way toward Charlie? He had known him for such a short time. He stared at his friend, his "buddy," long and hard then started to turn around and thought, "I should kneel and pray." He knelt and silently said, "Dear God, may the soul of Charlie Evans and all the souls of the faithful departed rest in peace." He repeated this over and then thought, "How cold."

He stopped and talked directly to his friend's soul. "Charlie, I'm so terribly sorry for what I've done to you! Why did I meddle in your life? Maybe you were happy with your way of life? Why didn't I just give you enough money for a bottle of 'Night Train Express'?"

As hard as Tim fought, he could not hold back the tears. He did not want whoever was sitting in those two chairs to see he had been crying.

He got up from his kneeler and went back and sat on one of the straight-back chairs, one chair removed from one of the other men.

He was able to get a good look at the men when he came back from the casket. They were obviously street people, very poorly dressed. The man on the other side wore shoes that were more stockings than shoes. He looked as if he were sleeping with his head on his chest.

Tim put his face in his hands for he felt the tears coming again.

"Ain't you Charlie's Buddy?"

"Charlie was a good friend of mine."

"No, I mean ain't you the one that got Charlie back on his feet?"

"Do you call that getting back on your feet?!" said Tim, pointing toward the casket.

"Hey, Mister, Charlie died a very happy man, a proud man!"

Tim's senses came completely to attention for he wanted to hear what this man was saying.

The man continued, "You oughtn't feel bad. What you did for Charlie was the greatest thing that ever happened to him! Lots of people think we like livin' on the street. We don't; it's hell! You're either cold, hot, hungry, or drunk, but never happy. The worst thing about it is you hate yourself because you know it's your fault even though you try to blame someone else. You don't think much of yourself, but that man over there in the casket felt when he died that he was somebody!"

The two sat there for a time as if in reflection.

The man again continued talking, "Tell you something else you did. You see there are five of us, and since you did this for Charlie, we all gave up drinking. So far only one of us has fallen off the wagon. He's back on now. We all like havin' a place to stay so we chipped in $60 to rent this old house."

"You mean that's where Charlie's $60 went?"

"Yeah, I'm the treasurer. I got his $60."

"You mean Charlie didn't have $60?! They killed him for nothing?"

"'At's right. They got nothing; we had it hid. The reason they tried to rob us was cause we had a place to stay and they thought we had some stash. They killed Charlie cause he was trying to protect us and kept fighting back!"

"Do you know who 'they' are?"

"No, just some heavies passing through. If it wasn't us it would've been some other poor downers like us. Robbery among street people happens a lot. They get pretty desperate, an' some of them have some expensive habits."

"Is there anything I can do to help you with the house?"

"No, maybe after we get settled, you can come over for a meal. Couple of us are pretty good cooks."

"I'd like that."

"Got any cigarettes?"

"No, I don't smoke."

"'At's OK. I'm tryin' to quit anyways. Think I'll leave now. See you at the funeral."

"Is that your friend there?"

"He must be a friend of Charlie's. He had lots of 'em."

Tim watched Charlie's friend leave, thinking, "Why didn't I get his name?" He sat there a moment then got up to leave, wondering what he should do about Charlie's other friend who was sleeping in the chair? "Leave him alone, I guess. He looks comfortable."

Charlie's funeral was a surprise. There were at least

thirty-five or forty people sitting and visiting in the room at Simms Mortuary waiting for the funeral to begin. Tim knew only a few: June his secretary, Pete Snyder from Maintenance, and Guy Rivers from Receiving. They were sitting together, so Tim joined them.

The crowd was made up of street people and a group of young people, late twenties to mid and late thirties, sitting together.

"I wonder if that's his family," thought Tim.

They didn't have long to wait. A pleasant, elderly, balding man in a dark suit came in and stood behind the lectern.

"Good afternoon, good friends of Charlie Evans. I'm Reverend Bill Merlo from the First Methodist Church." He stated that he didn't know Charlie. The minister talked about everyone having a value, referring to the Bible and how many times it addressed the "little ones," the sick, poor, and imprisoned. Then he said, "Since I didn't know Charlie, is there anyone here who'd like to share with us anything about Charlie?"

Without much hesitation, a pretty young lady with coal black hair and snapping black eyes, dressed in blue jeans and a denim shirt, walked over and stood by the lectern. Facing the people in the chairs, she stood, head bowed and hands clasped in front of her. She stood there for a long moment as if gathering her thoughts or her courage.

She looked up and said, "I knew and loved Charlie Evans. He ate most of his meals at the Kitchen except when he was working delivering hand bills or doing electrical work of some kind. We looked forward to seeing Charlie each day. He was truly a bright spot in our day.

"Charlie had a drinking problem, but I never saw him drunk. Out of respect for us, he would never drink before his afternoon meal. Charlie didn't like just coming for a free meal. He always wanted to do something for it, like emptying garbage cans, washing dishes, or scrubbing floors after the meal.

"Charlie and I used to sit and talk about our dreams. Charlie's dream was always the same dream, while mine would vary from day to day. His dream was more of a plan on how some day he would sober up and get off the street—how he would some day come back and help others leave the street. I always had the feeling that Charlie's dream would come true. Two weeks ago Charlie found a real job and he gave up drinking. He immediately started helping his friends to begin their dreams of getting off the streets."

She turned toward the casket and said, "I love you very much, Charlie, and I'm glad that your dream came true!"

While she returned to her seat, Reverend Merlo said, "Why don't we reflect silently on what we've just heard?"

Several handkerchiefs as well as sleeves were used for nose blowing and eye dabbing. The Reverend finished with appropriate readings, ending with the Lord's Prayer.

Two men from the mortuary came in and closed the casket and rolled it out of the room. There would be no internment as the body was to be cremated. Some of the people started to leave; others went back to visiting. Tim walked over to the young lady and said, "Good afternoon, I'm Tim Sorsen, a friend of Charlie's."

She looked up, extended her hand and said, "Oh, you're Charlie's Fairy Godfather. I'm Betty Osborne. This is great to get to meet you."

"When you said 'Kitchen,' is this the Catholic Worker's Soup Kitchen?"

"Yes."

"Charlie told me he ate there. You work there all the time?"

"No, I'm the Friday coordinator. I work every Friday."

"Do you get paid for this work?"

"It's all in the way you look at it. We don't get any money, but there's not enough money to equal the remuneration we do get."

"I'm sorry, that was a stupid question! How long have you been doing this?"

"Oh, I don't know, twelve maybe fifteen years now."

"You couldn't have been very old when you started. I can't believe anyone so young would give up so much of your life to help others."

"Like I say, the pay is good. If I didn't have to eat and have a place to sleep, I'd do it full time!"

"Hey, any chance I could get in on this high paying job?"

"Since Charlie gave you such a high recommendation, I think we can hire you," she said, eyes snapping.

"When do I start?"

"Come down any Friday morning or afternoon. We have two shifts. Eleven to about 2:30 and 2:30 to about 5:30. First shift prepares and cooks the meal, second shift finishes preparation, serves the meal along with doing dishes and scrubbing up after. I would think that you'd find the second shift more rewarding. You get the opportunity to meet and enjoy the company of those we serve."

"Thank you, Betty. See you Friday." He turned and looked for June and the others, but they had already left.

The following morning he arrived at his office, and Martin hailed him from the hallway, "Would you like to go over to Receiving and see the Ark before you start working?"

"Why, is there something special going on?"

"They have it all cleaned up and ready for showing.

Don't know when they're going to take it over to the museum. Thought we could take a look-see before it goes."

"Let me tell June where I'm going to be."

After Tim told June where he was going, she said, "Sir, you've heard the expression 'breathtaking.' When I say that's what you're going to find the Ark is, I mean you'll find that it'll literally take your breath away. Be prepared."

Tim and Martin made their way over to the Receiving building and to the Ark. It truly was the single most beautiful thing Tim had ever seen in his life! As June had warned, he was breathing in short gasps.

There were several people milling around the Ark. There was a mixture of voices and languages. The Ark was such a beautiful combination of shimmering gold and art that Tim couldn't take his eyes off it. If someone spoke to him, he would answer without looking at who he was talking to. If one of the workers walked in front of him, he would try, giraffe-like, to move his head to see around the obstacle.

He tore his eyes off the Ark to look for a chair. He wanted to sit down and just look at the Ark, but there were none. It was then that Tim noticed that these people were not SIMI employees. They must be the people from Israel who were to come and mother the Ark on its upcoming tour. At the moment, there were four workers dressed in clean white coveralls, one at each corner of the dazzling ornate chest. Cameras clicked and whirred. They each grasped the ends of the poles on either side and lifted the Ark a foot or so in the air. Two other white-clad workers pushed a platform topped with purple carpeting underneath. Tim found out that they were building a shipping container that would double as a showing stage while the Ark was on tour.

As Tim continued to look at the Ark, he started to get pangs of remorse as he noticed that they kept the Ark closed at all times. This very bad feeling continued and increased as he looked at the closed Ark. He turned quickly and started walking toward the door; Martin followed.

Tim returned to his office. He didn't sit at his desk but paced from window one to window two back to window one. He felt he had opened the sea valve to his own ship. He felt as if he had taken the only life jacket, leaving his friends with none.

In trying to analyze this feeling he thought, "I know that my meddling killed Charlie. I know I've let my own company and its employees down. I've let myself and my life's work down!" He paused in his rapid self-denunciation, thinking, "This isn't the cause of this terrible feeling of remorse. It's because I finally realized when I looked at that closed Ark that God and I aren't compatible! This is a terrible realization!"

Tim managed to finish his day behind his desk, trying specially to finish unfinished work and to mark ongoing work with notes and directions.

He spent his evening with Wally. They had a great dinner of curried shrimp over rice, followed by chocolate mousse. Tim spent most of the evening telling Wally about Charlie's funeral and how beautiful the Ark was now. Tim never mentioned his frustrations, but Wally, knowing his employer well, sensed his depression.

Chapter 10

*"Your ways O LORD make known to
me; teach me your paths"* (*Psalm* 25:4).

The following morning Tim asked Martin and June
to come into his office. He had June leave word with the
main office receptionist and telephone operator that
they were not to be disturbed. "June, put down your pad;
I'll tell you if we need to record anything of importance.
The rest of what I have to say, I think will be remembered.

"First, I brought a variety of breakfast rolls from
Martha's. Let's select one, get a cup of coffee and get
comfortable."

June reacted to the tray of rolls, "Mr. Sorsen, these are
sinful looking; look at this one, it must have at least a
week's worth of calories!"

Martin replied, "Good, I'll have that one."

They selected rolls, putting them on plates, and then
poured coffee. June and Martin looked uncomfortable.
Tim quickly said, "Please put your cups on the desk
before you spill hot coffee on yourselves.

"OK, what's all this about? I'd like to retire."

Martin quickly responded with, "Tim, now is not the
time to retire! It would cause panic among our stock-

holders, and the news media would play it up to the hilt! You're a news item right now!"

"I understand, Martin; let me finish. I realize that this is an inopportune time for me to retire. So what I'm going to do is make myself scarce for a time. I'm sure you've been aware that I've been having a hard time coping with the current events here at SIMI."

June replied, "It has affected us all, Sir."

"No, June, I must admit that I've been particularly affected by the Ark. I'm not in a state of mind capable of running a multi-million dollar company! It's very important that it be done now because there are decisions made daily that are important to this company that I don't want to make at this time!

"OK, what do we do about the media? Let's be deceptive and do it quietly. We'll call a Board of Directors meeting and at that meeting we'll make you, Martin, Executive Vice President. We'll explain to the members of the board that we're only preparing for the future when I do step down. In actuality, you will run the company. To help you, Martin, at this same meeting we'll make June a Vice President. Between you two, you'll have my proxies. June, you have some stock in the company, don't you?"

"Just a few shares, Sir. I've been considering converting some government bonds that George and I have to company stock."

"I think that would be a wise move, June. We'll adjust your salary to reflect your increased duties. Later on down the line you can leak the fact that I'm inactive. We can get by with this because I have controlling interest in the company."

"When do you plan on starting your retirement, Sir?"

"June, as Vice President and second in command at SIMI, I would appreciate it if you would call me 'Tim.'

As to when I'm going to start my retirement, let me ask you, what time is it?"

"It's 9:03, Sir . . . I'm sorry, Tim."

"OK, I'm leaving in a few minutes, because I'm going to start my retirement by going to church."

"It's Tuesday morning. Is this a special day or something?"

"No, I just like going to church at 10:30 on Tuesday mornings." Neither Martin nor June thought they would ask him why, they just left it lie.

Tim continued, "I expect you'll have questions from time to time, so call me anytime. I'll also be in to sign whatever needs my signature once or twice a week. Please use my office and desk. I have nothing personal in either."

He stood to go. June and Martin were at a loss for something to say. As he approached the door, June said, "Say a prayer for Martin and me, Tim."

He headed the Mercedes toward Forest Park and Our Lady of the Forest. Instead of going right into the church as he did before, he walked around the flower beds which were on every side of the church. In one of the flower beds he saw a black lump. The lump moved from time to time, so Tim walked over to investigate. It was the little ancient priest he had met on his first visit.

"Good morning, Father."

The lump looked up and smiled, a very pleasant smile, almost as if he had been expecting him.

"Good morning to you. Are you selling something? If you are, remember that God has already given us everything we need." Father raised his hand for help to get to his feet.

While Father was trying to unkink his back and stand

up straight, Tim said, "No Father, I'm not selling anything. I came here to visit."

"Don't tell me–you came here to visit God. I remember you. You were here once before to talk to God, and I think I know who you are, too. You're that fellow who runs a machine company, the one who found the Ark."

"You have a good memory, and you do have the right man. I'm Tim Sorsen."

"Don't remember if I introduced myself last time. I'm Father Bob. If you'd like to visit the church, just go push the bell at the office door. The secretary will let you in."

"No, Father, I would like to visit with you."

"Great! Nobody wants to visit with me anymore. They say I'm too old and too set in my ways. I'll have to warn you though, that if you're a right-wing Republican, I'll cut the visit short. Do you like tea?"

"I'm afraid I am a Republican, but I don't know if I belong to the right wing, and I do like tea."

"Let's go inside, have some tea, and talk. The Lord has told me I have to counsel everyone, even Republicans."

They sat in a modern kitchen at a small table with four place mats and three straight-back chairs. Father put three tea bags in a tea pot and waited for the tea kettle to whistle. He said he didn't want to sit down until the water was hot.

While they were waiting, Tim said, "I don't know when I've seen prettier flowers. Your flower beds are gorgeous!"

"Yes, they are. They're for a gorgeous Lady. They're for the Holy Mother." Father took the whistling tea kettle and filled the tea pot, put it on the table between them, and sat down. He looked at Tim and waited for whatever he might have to say.

"Father, it helps that you know who I am because you already know part of my problem. It's the Ark and the effect it's had on me and the effect it's had on my life."

"I'm not surprised. Sometimes people who go to the Holy Land are affected by the fact that the place really exists, and that it's not a fairy tale from the Bible."

"It's a little more than that, Father. You see, I invited God to come and be my constant Companion!"

"Oh my! That is different. What made you think you were man enough to handle that?"

"I didn't realize how difficult it would be, and you're right, I wasn't man enough to handle it."

"Did God berate you or condemn you?"

"No, He advised me, and I found His advice affecting my life adversely. And this effect carried over to my business, friends, and associates."

"When you say adversely, do you mean that God gave you bad advice?"

"No, I guess not."

"How then did God fault the companionship?"

"He demanded too much."

"Give me an example."

"He wanted me to ignore the ways of man."

"Were the ways of man correct ways that He questioned?"

"Not exactly correct but just doing things that they've been doing for thousands of years. They were just being human."

Father did not respond, he just sipped his tea and smiled.

Tim smiled also and said, "I know what you just did, Father. You let me hang myself with my own rope. I guess my problem is even bigger than I thought. What all this means then is that I'm not acceptable to God!"

"Hold on there! You are going the wrong way, Corrigan. Review: did God ever tell you or indicate you were not acceptable to Him?"

"No."

"No, of course not. How old are you; what's your first name?"

"Tim, I'm sixty-two."

"Pretty set in your ways?"

"Yes, I guess you would say I am."

"Well, God is even more set in His ways, but He makes allowances for you and me. I gather that this thinking is new to you, at least thinking at this depth?" Tim nodded.

"My advice to you would be to slow down. Approach your relationship with God on a day to day basis. Question your thoughts and deeds before you have or do them. Ask yourself, 'What would Jesus think about this? Is this what He would do or say?'

"I'd say you're not ready to have God as a constant Companion. Condition yourself, do things as often as you can to please God, until it becomes habit.

"If you really want to please God, there is a sure way to His heart–take on duties for the good of society. Are you aware that the social justice theme threads its way throughout the Bible. The thread is more like a steel cable. If we ministers and priests were to talk proportionately about what's in the Bible, three weeks a month or nine months a year, we would talk about social justice. God really loves the sick, the poor, and the downtrodden. Look for the Lord in these people!

"Use any method you choose, but you must make pleasing God a habit. It will be hard at first, but remember that most of what you do already pleases Him. None of us can compare ourselves to God. If we did this, we'd feel very miserable. We can, however, head ourselves in the right direction.

"To what do you credit your successes in life, Tim?"

"Being first, beating my competition."

"Typical first world attitude. I hope you can apply your formula to Christ's rule, 'If anyone wishes to be first, he shall be last of all and the servant of all.'"

Father sipped his tea; Tim looked into his tea cup and beyond. He had heard this quote many times, but this was the first time he **heard** it!

"Tim, I believe your relationship with God was and is much stronger than you thought. Try developing it at a pace you can handle.

"Oh yes, another thing, Tim: it would help if you were to become a Democrat."

"Thank you, Father. I feel much better. I admit I was feeling pretty low. As for becoming a Democrat, I think I'll try going through the Pearly Gates as a Republican."

"You do make it hard on yourself," Father said as he refreshed their tea.

Tim spent the better part of an hour in pleasant conversation, telling Father about his experience with the Ark, listening to Father about his experience with life and his own relationship with God. The result was that he felt much better about himself and life than he did when he came.

"Thank you so much for time and counsel. I enjoyed my visit very much."

"I, too, enjoyed the visit. I hope you will come back."

"You can count on it."

Chapter 11

"Give to the hungry some of your bread, and to the naked some of your clothing. Whatever you have left over, give away as alms; and do not begrudge the alms you give" (*Tobit* 4:16).

Two-thirty p.m. Friday found Tim at the Catholic Worker's Soup Kitchen. His first impression was not good. It was a very old squat building that had housed some kind of business in the past. It had two large windows in the front, like a store front, with a door in the middle. He walked into an area that might have been an office, now filled with boxes and crates of vegetables, fruit, potatoes, and other fresh produce. There were two ladies and a man separating some not-so-fresh peaches, putting some in a new box and some in a garbage can. They smiled and greeted Tim as he passed through.

From there he went into the kitchen area which had a small room off to the side with large stainless steel sinks. Tim thought, "This is where they do the dishes." The walls leading to the kitchen from the front area were lined with six refrigerators, freezers, cupboards, or shelves. Wherever there was an open place along the wall there were utensils hanging from nails. The kitchen had a large gas stove with two large ovens. It looked to be of commercial quality, in good repair.

From the kitchen one could go into the largest room, an old garage with a garage door and a regular door on the back side. The masonry walls were painted white with a small amount of religious graffiti. The cement floors looked squeaky clean, showing no signs that it had ever been used as a garage. This room had eight folding tables with five folding chairs to each side of each table. There was a strong smell of bleach throughout the ramshackle building.

The place was buzzing with activity. Three large, fifteen-gallon, stainless steel kettles were on the stove top being stirred by a man with what looked like a canoe paddle. In the room with the large sinks, people were washing and sorting lettuce and cutting tomatoes. In between the front area and the kitchen they were peeling hard-boiled eggs.

Someone slapped him on the back and said, "Hey, Sorsen, I see you made it."

It was Betty Osborne.

"You have a good memory for names."

"Comes from liking people. Want something to do?"

"You bet."

"OK, why don't you help Sally and Tom here peel eggs. Sally, Tom, this is Tim. Make sure he works hard."

Tim started cracking and peeling the hard-boiled eggs. "There must be a gross in here," he said.

Sally asked, "Are you from a group?"

"No, I just heard about the Kitchen and decided to come down."

"Wonderful, you'll love it. Tom and I belong to 'Our Lady of the Forest' and we come down once a month on Fridays."

"Lovely church. I just met your pastor, Father Bob."

"Oh, Father Bob isn't the pastor. Father Bob's retired. He just helps around the parish and takes care of the flower beds. He's going to stay at the parish as long as he can take care of himself."

Tim smiled both inwardly and outwardly.

They finished peeling the eggs and somebody said, "It's prayer time."

Tim asked, "Thought they didn't pray or preach here at the Kitchen?"

"Oh, it's not a formal prayer; we just take a moment to prepare ourselves to serve those who will eat here today." They all went into the dining area and formed a circle by holding hands.

Betty said, "Would anyone like to say the prayer?"

Tim bowed his head for fear they would call on him. A voice of one of the men began, "Dear Lord, we thank You for this opportunity of meeting old friends and greeting new friends today. Please help us get to know our old friends better and to quickly get acquainted with new friends. Keep us aware that these burdened people could be our father, mother, brother, sister, or our very selves, if it were not for Your graces. We ask You, please, make us alert to recognize You, for we know You will be in the line with those we serve today! Amen."

Betty said, "Does everybody have jobs? I need someone to serve soup and someone for the salad. Tim, you're new, why don't you serve the soup. Get right into the thick of things." She motioned him over to a counter which had large containers of bread, salad, bananas, boiled eggs, and cake. Sitting on a short stool at the end of the counter was a steaming fifteen-gallon kettle of hot soup. There was a large stainless steel ladle on the end of the counter along with two large stacks of soup bowls.

The servers got behind the counters, and the ones who would be serving the coffee, tea, and water readied themselves. Everyone was talking happily at the same time.

They opened the small door, and in came the hungry. Now Tim had seen tramps, bums, and street people before, but usually one or two at a time. This was much different for he soon became surrounded by them en masse. Some were sullen, some were rude, others were polite, happy, and many said, "Thank you," with eye contact and a smile. He was surprised to see some women and even families with children there.

The soup was hardy with very little broth. He heard quite a few ask for more eggs; they were told they would have to wait until everyone was served. If there were some left over, they would be welcome to them. Same held true for the cake. Tim asked, "Do they only get one bowl of soup, too?"

The lady serving the cake said, "Oh no, they can have as much soup and bread as they want. They will be coming back for seconds and thirds, you'll see."

Tim felt good, elated. He tried to make eye contact with each person to whom he served a bowl of soup. He knew if he tried to describe what he was seeing he could not. Yes, many looked dirty. Yes, some were drunk. No, he did not feel like shooing them away like dirty flies. He felt drawn to them, wondering why he was so lucky to be on this side of the counter. He wondered if he would have been strong enough to deal with the life that was dealt to them!

"Can I just have some broth?" said a man standing in front of Tim with a tray that had nothing but bread on it. "That's going to be hard; this soup is really thick."

"I ain't got no teeth. I can't eat the thick part."

"Let me see what I can do," he said trying to get a bowl of just broth.

"Betty came by and patted the man on the back saying, "Hi, Sam. How are you today?"

"Fine, Betty. Got me a couple of jobs this week."

"Keep it up, Sam. You'll have those teeth in no time."

Tim handed Sam his bowl of broth.

He was a little baldheaded man with rather large ears. It was obvious that he had no teeth, with his cheeks and mouth caved in. Sam was wearing a three sizes too big, red flannel shirt, oversized, worn, blue jeans, held up with a belt that was a foot too long. He was wearing fairly new hiking boots that looked like they fit. Sam looked like a Norman Rockwell creation of a little man in a soup line.

"Thank you, Mister. Hope I didn't hold up the line too much."

"If you want more, Sam, come back."

The people kept coming. As soon as someone finished someone else would take their place at the tables. Betty came up and put her hand on Tim's shoulder. "Why don't you take a break. We have a big crew today. Go out to the tables and talk to the people. Make them feel at home." She took the ladle from him and handed it to Tom who was standing by her side.

Tim walked among the eaters, embarrassed at first, not knowing what to say or do. "Wouldn't you be more comfortable eating without that big backpack on?"

"I can't watch it and eat, too."

"We'll watch it for you. Here let me help you get it off." He put the pack up against the wall close to where the ladies were serving coffee and tea.

To another he said, "Would you like some more soup?"

"You betcha, 'at's good soup. Any chance you could get me another piece of cake?"

Tim took the empty bowl to Tom, who refilled it. He

turned to the lady who was serving cake and said, "I'll take my piece of cake, please." All of a sudden he realized that he didn't have a tray or any place to put the cake so he quickly put out his hand. She smiled and filled the hand. He returned with the soup and cake.

There sat Sam, sopping up the last of his broth with bread. "Sam, you want some more broth?"

"Yeah," said Sam, surprised. "About a half a bowl will do."

Tom, who knew how to get broth from the soup by pushing the ladle into the soup just far enough to let broth flow over the top of the ladle, quickly filled the bowl. Tim grabbed as much bread as he could hold in one hand. "Here you go, Sam."

"Thanks, Mister. I could of gotten it."

"Enjoy your soup, Sam."

Sam was sitting on one side at the end of the table. Tim knelt down in the aisle for they did not seat anyone on the ends of the tables.

"Sam, I heard you tell Betty that you got a couple of jobs. What do you do?"

"Anything." He finished gumming some bread and continued, "Those of us that don't have regular jobs stand around down by the old Russel Building at 8th and Strand, and people come by and pick us up for odd jobs. They pay us cash when we finish."

"Isn't that illegal?"

"No, we don't do nothin' wrong."

Tim did not explain why it was probably illegal. "You told Betty that you were trying to get some teeth."

"Yeah."

"How long have you been without teeth?"

"Oh, I don't know, four or five years now. I had the money for a set of choppers once, but my daughter's old car broke down and she had to get another one. Now I got over \$300 saved. Well, I don't exactly have it—my daughter's hot water heater sprang a leak and she had to get a new one, but she's going to pay me back soon as she can."

"You say that is by the old Russel Building?"

"Yeah."

"Will you be there Monday?"

"Yeah, I s'pose so."

"I might have something for you to do, Sam."

Tim felt a hand on his shoulder and looked up. It was Charlie's friend who he had met at the funeral home.

"Hello, how are you? You know, I don't think I got your name before?"

"It's Dewayne, Dewayne Fortney."

"Dewayne, I'm Tim."

"Hi, Tim. I saw you here and thought I'd say 'Hello.'"

"I'm glad you did. How's that house coming?"

"Well, we got it rented, but the city won't let us move in until we get utilities. They say it wouldn't be sanitary."

"Can you get your money back?"

"No, they say they don't refund rent."

"Who are 'they'?"

"The Auburn Company."

"The Auburn Company? Are you sure?"

"Yeah, it's the Auburn Company. We paid in advance; we're supposed to move in on the first."

"I know that company. Let me see what can be done. What's the address of the house?"

"1201 Meeker."

"I don't have anything to write with, but I'll remember—1201 Meeker. How will I be able to get ahold of you?"

"Oh, we're still in number 417; we still have eight days left."

"I'll be in touch the first of the week."

"We thank you, Tim, but remember, it ain't like sixty bucks is a lot of money."

"It is when it's your last sixty bucks!"

"Yeah, you got that right. You're an all right guy, Tim."

Betty took hold of Tim's arms just above the elbows with an unbelievably firm grip, black eyes snapping above a pleasant smile. "Hey, Mister Tim, you really got into this thing big. Most people find it hard to talk to my dear friends who come here to the Kitchen to eat. They like you! Please say you're coming back."

"You couldn't keep me away! I don't know when I've had such a great feeling. I'm sixty-two years old and finally finding out what's really meant when we say it's better to give than receive. What actually happens is you end up receiving more than you give. The harder you try to give, the more you receive!"

"Speaking of receiving, Tim, here's a mop. Fun time's over."

Tim propped his two pillows up on his bed one behind the other and sat up in his bed with hands behind his head with a pleased smile on his face. This smile was different from all his other smiles. This was not a smile from where the body stores humor, not a smile from recognition, or a deceptive smile, but a smile from deep within where real happiness comes from—the tiny spot that emits waves of satisfaction. The last time he used this particular smile was when he was elected President of Sacred Heart of Jesus High School's Student Council.

Tim and his smile were greeted by Wally the following morning. "My, you look pleased this morning; did you find out you were having Eggs Goldenrod this morning?"

"I didn't, but I do feel good. Good morning, Wally."

"Good morning, Sir. I'm afraid that the morning paper may dampen your spirits a bit."

"Oh, no, what now?" Sitting down he reached for the *News*.

The headlines read, "**Israel Cancels Ark's Tour**," followed by:

> Israel canceled the Ark of the Covenant's tour after the second day. The tour was mobbed by unbelievably large crowds! The crowds were calm and manageable for the most part. Only their size was a problem. Even considering the size of the crowd, police, security, staff, and volunteers were coping.
>
> What brought about Israel's decision to cancel the tour was that on day one there were five heart attacks–three in the building containing the Ark, two in waiting lines. Three of the attacks were fatal. Day two brought another four heart attacks–two in the proximity of the Ark, one in the waiting lines, and one on a shuttle bus, with two fatalities.
>
> Why this abnormal number of attacks? There are several theories, one that it is not unusual. If you were to again put the same number of people in the same confined space for the same length of time, you would have the same results. Another theory is the stress of the anticipation of seeing the Ark and the stress of actually seeing it, combined with the effort of waiting in a long line, were to blame. Then there are those who say that just being close to the Holy Ark was too much for these individuals.

Bishop Jerome was asked if there could be any supernatural connection. He said there could be, but he doubted that there was. He said that he also believed the large crowd and stress to be the causes.

One of the people who had an attack was interviewed. A forty-nine-year-old woman, who wished her name withheld, said that she merely panicked because of the crowd, and she could not escape to leave.

The story was continued on 9A.

Tim said, "Why wasn't this on the news before?"

"It was, Sir. It was on the news several times, but you've been so busy you missed it. I didn't want to tell you because I think you've had enough Ark."

"You got that right, but when is all of this going to stop?"

"For right now it's going to stop while you eat this Eggs Goldenrod! You know you have to eat it while it's still hot."

"Thanks, Wally. Looks delicious."

After breakfast, Tim said, "I'm going to the mall. Anything you need?"

"A new wardrobe would be nice."

"Sure, Wally. I'll be back for lunch."

He went to the Westward Department Store to look for jeans. He didn't have any except some old ones he used for painting and the like. If he remembered right, they were hip huggers with bell bottoms. He wanted some that hugged more than his hips. Tim wanted the jeans to wear to the Kitchen. He was surprised at the price of jeans. "My God, I can buy good dress pants cheaper than that!"

He wasn't sure if he should buy them the right size or a size bigger because he had heard that they shrunk when they were washed. He found a young sales clerk and asked her.

"Yes and no," she said. "Some are pre-washed and some are not. Here are some pre-washed, nice looking, full-cut jeans. Why don't you find your size and try them on. The dressing room's right here."

"Thanks, I will."

Tim put on the jeans and started out of the dressing room, stopping to take his wallet with him. Coming out of the dressing room he found a mirror. He thought the jeans looked like they fit pretty good.

The young clerk said, "Oh yes, they fit great, but when you wear them forget the wallet. That way we can see your cute butt." A red-faced Tim returned to the dressing room. He was surprised by his own embarrassment. He was not usually so sensitive. But now he sensed a more accute awareness of the impropriety of the clerk's remark than he would have in times past.

He bought two pair of jeans and two denim shirts and went over to the shoe department and bought a pair of name-brand running shoes.

He returned to his car and was headed home when all of a sudden he pulled over to the curb and got the city map out of the glove compartment. "Where the heck is Meeker Street anyway?" It was hard to find because it was only four blocks long. He knew the area but was surprised that there would be any homes in this industrial area.

Fifteen minutes later Tim was parked on Meeker Street in front of 1201. "What in hell is holding it up?" he thought. It was a ramshackle with some of the windows busted out, some covered with pieces from brown corrugated boxes. There was a "For Rent" sign hanging cockeyed on the front porch bannister.

He went up the porch stairs and tried the door; it was open. Inside was as bad as the outside. Plain light fixtures hung from the ceilings. The walls were a dirty gray. He could not tell if the surface was paper, paint, or plaster. The floors were covered with very worn and broken linoleum. Tim thought, "I haven't seen linoleum since I was a kid." The sinks, bathtub, and stool, which were once white porcelain, were now grayish black and rust colored with no white showing.

Tim went back outside and turned around to look at the house. He became aware that there was a man sitting on the porch of the house next door.

"If you're lookin' fer a house to rent, that one's already rented." The man started walking toward the fence separating the two houses.

"Yes, I know. The people who rented it wanted me to look at it for them."

"Ain't much. The Browns pretty well trashed the place."

"The Browns—is that who lived here before?"

"Yeah, there was a whole batch of 'em. None of 'em had jobs, and they just sat around drinkin' an' smokin' an' fightin'. The old lady an' I were sure glad when they moved out.

"Don't know much about the new renters. I only met one of 'em, an' I'm sure he ain't no banker. You say you know them? They ain't going to sell dope or run a whore house or nothin', are they?"

"No, they're just five men who're homeless and need a home."

"Boy, that don't sound none too good! I s'pose the lazy bastards don't have no jobs either?"

"Well, they're going to have to pay the rent or they won't be here."

"Yeah. Well, I say 'live and let live.' If they don't bother me, I won't bother them."

"You'll get along fine. Got to run. See you later."

"Nice wheels you got there."

"Thanks."

Sunday after lunch Tim picked up the phone and called his neighbor, Dr. George Luptin. "Hello, Marge. Is George there?"

"That you, Tim? He's here somewhere. He hides from me, you know. Hang on."

"Hello, Tim."

"Hello, George. I need your help."

"Hey, remember me. I got a sore back and a weak heart!"

"I got a friend who needs false teeth."

"Good. I can use the business; all I do is stand around all day."

"I know you're busy George, but this guy's gone without teeth for five years!"

"Why, they're not that hard to get . . . ?"

"He doesn't have any money!"

"Oh, I see. You want a freebie."

"No! No! I'll pay you, but he'll need kind of special treatment."

"What kind of special treatment?"

"Well, the old guy is old."

"Most old guys are old!"

"George, I'm not sure what I mean. It's just that I don't think the old guy is up to coming in for a lot of visits to the dentist's chair."

"Tim, if this 'old guy' has gone five years without any

teeth, then he sure knows what misery is. I don't think a lot of visits is going to be any problem because, after five years without teeth, his gums should be in great shape for plates. With one or two visits, we'll give the 'old guy' a dazzling smile. He may have to come back for adjustments if he develops any sore spots in his mouth. Again, if this guy can handle not having teeth for five years, he can handle this. Who is he?"

"His name is Sam."

"Sam who?"

"I don't know his last name."

"He work for you?"

"No, I met him at the Soup Kitchen."

"Things that bad at SIMI, Tim?"

"I just found out about the place and thought I'd go down and help out. You should go down; it gives you a great feeling."

"Marge goes down regularly and has been trying to get me to go. I'll get around to it sooner or later."

"How are we going to handle this, George? I was hoping that we could get the old fellow taken care of pretty soon."

"If you think I'm coming in today, you're crazier than I think you are! I do have a busy practice, but give Esther a call in the morning. I'll talk to her. We have several cancellations a day, but–like the airlines–we overbook. We also use the cancellation time for emergencies. With some luck we can get your Sam in Monday."

"Hey, that would be great! I don't know what to say."

"'Goodbye' would be nice."

"Thanks, George!" Dial tone.

Tim hung up the phone and went to the kitchen wearing that same smile he had found Friday. He poured a juice glass of V8 and went back into the den, looked up William Auburn's number, and dialed. "Is Bill there?"

"Who may I say is calling?"

"Tell Bill that Tim Sorsen would like to talk to him."

"Just a moment, please."

"Tim, how's my best customer?"

"I'm fine, Bill. Sorry to bother your weekend, but I kind of got involved in something, and I need your help."

"You know I'll help if I can, Tim."

"A group of men who I met at the Catholic Worker's Soup Kitchen have rented a house on Meeker Street, and it's in such poor repair the city won't let them move in."

"Don't know how I could help you there, Tim."

"They said that the homes belong to the Auburn Company."

"You say that house is on Meeker Street? Isn't that all industrial down there?"

"Yes, but there are three or four blocks of homes on Meeker. I was there yesterday."

"Boy, I don't know, Tim. We've picked up some property around town—got to diversify, you know—but that doesn't sound familiar. Don't get me wrong; it could be ours. I just don't remember it. I'll sure find out though. If it's ours, what did you want me to do? Refund their rent money or what?"

"No, Bill. I'd like to buy it."

"Tim I'm thinking that if this property does belong to Auburn, we wouldn't have bought just one house. We probably bought a whole tract of homes. We're not interested in residential homes as such. We do have some that we rent until we can develop the property for industrial use. Now this house may be smack dab in the middle of such a project."

"Don't think so, Bill. This house is the first house on Meeker Street; it's a corner house."

"If we own this house, how bad do you want it, Tim?"

"Bad enough to call and ask you!"

"Of course, you know I can't turn you down."

"Bill, I'm not trying to pressure you because of the amount of business my company does with yours. I'm just asking. I want to pay a fair price."

"Tim, I'll find out first thing Monday morning and give you a call."

"I'll be out Monday morning. Why don't I give you a call. OK?"

"Fine, Tim. How were those conversions on the Ford trucks we did for you last month?"

"First class, as always. Martin tells me there'll be more. I'll let you get back to your Sunday, Bill."

"I'll look for your call, Tim."

He hung up the phone thinking, "Would Jesus have done that?" He knew he was pressuring Bill to sell him that house. Still, that smile returned, but on close inspection it had a slight devilish slant to it. As he reached for his V8 he thought, "I'm meddling again. Maybe Sam won't want to go to the dentist. Just buying the house doesn't solve Dewayne's and his friends' problems."

Chapter 12

"He who does a kindness is remembered afterward; when he falls, he finds a support" (*Sirach* 3:30).

Monday morning Tim made a quick stop at SIMI, signed some papers, and had a brief meeting with Martin and June. He called Esther at George Luptin's office and was told, "Bring your Mister Sam in anytime, and we'll work him in."

Ten-thirty found him in front of the old Russel Building looking for Sam. He didn't see him but decided to drive around the block and make sure he hadn't missed him among the twenty or so men standing there. Sure enough, he was there, sitting in a doorway behind some men. He stopped, rolled down the window, and motioned to him. Sam pointed to himself to make sure it was him that Tim wanted. One of the other men said, "Hey, I can outwork that little guy!" Sam walked over to the car and looked in before he recognized Tim.

"Oh, you're the guy from the Kitchen."
"Good morning, Sam. Please get in."
As he drove through traffic he said, "I don't have a job

157

for you, Sam. We're going to a dentist friend of mine and get you some teeth!"

"Oh, wow! I don't know about this!"

"You do want false teeth, don't you?"

"Oh yeah, yeah ! It's just that this is all kind of scary. Who are you anyway? I ain't got no money."

"My name is Tim Sorsen. The dentist doesn't want any money. We just thought that after five years without, you deserved to get some teeth."

"I feel kind of funny. What'll they have to do, drill an' all that stuff?"

"No, just make a cast of your mouth."

"What's a cast?"

"Oh, it's just some stuff they put in your mouth to make a mold for the people who make the teeth."

"I thought that the teeth just came in different sizes."

"Not that simple, Sam."

"I ain't no scaredy-cat or nothin', it's just that I want to know what I'm getting into."

"I don't think he's going to do anything that hurts."

"Wonder if I should tell my wife what I'm doin'?"

"Why don't you just surprise her, Sam?"

"Yeah, hey that's a great idea. She'll really be surprised!"

"I didn't see your wife at the Kitchen, did I?"

"Nope she babysits some neighbor's kids an' their folks feed her. We get Social Security, but it don't last the whole month, an' we run out of food an' stuff if I don't get enough work."

"Here we are, Sam," Tim said as he pulled into Dr. Luptin's parking lot.

They went inside. Esther said, "Good morning, Tim. This must be Sam. Good morning, Sam."

"Morning, Ma'am. I wanna thank you for what you're doing for me."

"We like doing it, Sam. Have a seat and I'll get you in to see the doctor very shortly."

Tim picked up a weekly news magazine and started leafing through it. Sam picked up another magazine, and after a couple of minutes, Tim heard the tearing of paper and could tell from his peripheral vision that Sam was tearing coupons from the magazine.

Tim returned Sam to the Russel Building at one o'clock, after they had stopped at Denny's for a bowl of tomato soup and a dish of ice cream. George had made a cast for the plates to be made from and told him to come back Thursday at 5:00 p.m. Sam said he would have his daughter take him there.

Getting out of the car, Sam turned back and stuck his hand in toward Tim.

"Mister, you're some kind of a guy. I sure do thank you!"

"See you at the Kitchen, Sam."

A moment later one of two young men in a car in the opposite lane of traffic from Tim, said to the other, "Look at that old guy over there smiling; he must really like driving that Mercedes!"

Tim returned to his home and den. He called Bill Auburn's office.

"Mr. Auburn is out of the office. May I take a message?"

"This is Tim Sorsen. When do you expect Bill back?"

"He'll be gone for the rest of the day, but he was expecting your call and left a message for you, Mr. Sorsen. He said that the property was yours. You are to have it appraised, deduct the rent money the men have paid, and send us a check. He also said you might want to have your attorney handle the transaction."

"Thank Bill for me, and thanks for your help."

Tim sat down to the table, martini in hand, and said, "Wally, you have outdone yourself tonight. Looks and smells like 'Hens Elegant.'"

"I hope they taste as good as they look and smell."

Tim spent the rest of the dinner hour telling Wally about his day and the events that led up to them.

Wally's response was slow, as if he were choosing his words carefully. "Sir, I know you've always been a good person, but lately it seems I'm getting a look at a different you. God must be awfully pleased with you!"

"On that score, I'm not sure, Wally."

"Did you hear the latest on the Ark?"

"Is it in the paper?" Tim asked, reaching for the paper.

"No. It must have happened too late for the paper. It was on the six o'clock news on Channel 4. It seems that Israel is going to send the Ark back to SIMI to be prepared for shipping and to give them time to make security arrangements."

"You're kidding."

"No, Sir. It said your Mr. Mills made the arrangements to emphasize the good relations between Israel, the United States, and SIMI."

"Sounds like Martin is in there pitchin'! I just talked to him this morning and he didn't say anything about this." Tim thought to himself, "Maybe I ought to call Martin? No, Sorsen, butt out! Martin is running the show now."

He took his coffee and the paper into the den. He read through rehashed world news where people were at odds with their governments and governments were at odds with other governments.

Page five had a filler that caught his eye. The heading read: "**Social concerns latest rage.**"

> People involved in the works of social jus-
> tice are reporting a big surge in volunteers,
> money, food, and clothing to these organiza-
> tions. A large number of individual acts of
> charity are being reported by the media.
>
> The cause of this phenomenon is
> unknown and is not isolated to the US. The
> rise has also been reported in Europe and
> Asia. Some suggest that the rise coincides
> with the discovery of the Ark of the
> Covenant in a machinery company ware-
> house in the US. Others dismiss this and say
> it is merely a sign of the times.

Tim stopped reading and looked out the window,
watching the wind move the leaves on the trees, and he
thought about this article. He then went back to his
paper. He perked up when he recognized the name Perry
Ulrich on page eleven.

It was a very small article. It stated Perry resigned his
position with the city. It also said that the property in
Perry's wife's mother's name will be sold to the city for
common value. The article also stated the District Attorney said there would be nothing to gain for the Grand
Jury to pursue the matter any further.

"That's good news," he thought.

Tuesday morning found Tim at the Lincoln Hotel,
knocking on the door of number 417. Dewayne opened
the door wearing only an undershirt and a pair of pants.
There was one man in the bed and another sitting on a
chair putting on his shoes.

"Hi, Tim. Come on in."

"He stepped just inside the door saying, "You fellows
up for some breakfast?"

"We don't often eat no breakfast, but coffee and a grease ring sure does sound good!" The man in the bed sat up and grinned sheepishly at Tim.

"I want to talk to you about your house on Meeker Street. I'll wait for you down in the lobby."

"We'll be down in a jiff."

For Tim, waiting in the lobby was like living in another world, watching the people of the hotel. He wondered why so many were asleep in chairs if they had rooms. Others read papers, and a few were watching television with the sound turned way up. Not as many looked at Tim in his jeans as they did when he wore a business suit.

The three men came down looking almost as if they had just stepped out of a shower or tub, hair slicked down, and not too badly dressed.

"This here's Blair, and he's Tommy."

"Nice to meet you fellows," Tim said and shook their hands. "Any place we can get some breakfast?"

The men looked at each other for a moment.

"There's the Front Street Cafe across the street. Tommy sometimes washes dishes there."

The four men walked across the street to the cafe. The cafe was quite modern, showing only a little wear here and there. The dining area was almost square with counter and stools along two walls, booths along the other walls, and tables in the center. Menus and condiments were in the center of each table and on the counters. There were also large menus on the walls behind the counters. Waylon and Willie were being accompanied by clattering dishes and the thirty-odd customers' yammering. A smell, not offensive, of disinfectant and cooking bacon was in the air. Which one you smelled would depend on how hungry you were.

They sat in a booth by the front window. Tim handed menus around. There were only three; he shared one with Blair.

Dewayne said, "We ain't got no money. Least wise, not none that we can spend."

"No, no, I'll buy breakfast."

Tommy said, "You mean a regular breakfast like eggs and stuff?"

"Order anything you want, Tommy."

The waitress brought their breakfast and had a hard time getting it all on the table.

"I thought there was five of you?"

"There was five, but Charlie's gone an' Frank's at work. Frank got a job carrying hod on a construction job for about a week."

"I went over and saw your house. Frankly, it's not much of a house!"

"Mister, when you ain't got no home, that there house is a beautiful castle!"

"You can't live in it the way it is!"

"Hey, Blair, show Tim our plans."

Blair was too busy trying to decide what to put on his fork—egg, sausage, pancake, or hash browns. All of a sudden he responded, put down his fork and reached inside his shirt taking out several 8½ by 11 unfolded sheets of white paper with drawings and sketches. He looked for a place to put them down. Tim quickly took the papers and said, "Go ahead and eat your meal; we'll look at these when we get the table cleaned."

He couldn't resist looking, and leafed through the papers not believing what he saw. He remembered the ramshackle house and was now looking at a sketch of that house in color, by crayon, in perfect repair. It was a doll house! The other papers were exterior and interior plans with dimensions to the fraction of an inch. Plumbing and electrical outlets were indicated.

"You fellows have put a lot of thought into this thing," Tim said as he put the papers on a shelf between the booth and the window.

"Fixin' that ol' house up would make us feel like we fixed up five ol' bums, too. It's a dream we share about doin' somethin'. Right now it don't look like we's goin' to get a chance to do it though."

"Let's talk about that later. Right now I want to know how you plan to get this job done."

"Mister, people throw away good stuff. We can go to the garbage dump and get good plumbing fixtures, toilets, sinks, tubs, wiring, switches, lumber, and trim. You can't believe what people throw away. Right now we have a problem with window glass. We need to come up with some money for that, but if we get work enough, we should be able to swing that and still have enough for rent and utilities."

"But, Dewayne, you're only going to rent this place. You'll just be helping the landlord!"

"No, we'll be helpin' ourselves, and when the landlord sees what we've done, he'll want us to stay an' take care of the place."

"Or he could sell the place and make a big profit or charge you more rent because the place is so nice!"

"We talked about that and decided fixin' that place up would be good for us, an' if that happens we'll find another place. We wants us a home!"

"Well, guys, I have something to tell you, and I hope you're not mad at me for meddling in your affairs, but I bought that house."

"Oh," Dewayne said, "Does that mean we can't rent her or fix her up?"

"No! That means you can rent it and fix it up! You had better start looking for sinks and toilets and whatever else you need to fix it up."

"We already got a kitchen sink, bathtub, an' a toilet an some other stuff stashed away!"

"OK, I'll get the lights, water, and gas turned on. I'll also get a permit for remodeling today. Tomorrow we'll pick up the window glass."

"So OK, but all of us can't work on her every day. We got to work. You know that we gets jobs. Sometimes we get two or three jobs a week. But there'll always be a couple of us workin' on her."

Blair was looking at everybody's plates to make sure all the food was gone.

"I suggest you fellows get started on your new home. As an added incentive I'll go a step further. If you fellows each pay me $60 a month for four years, the house will be yours!"

Blair said, "I don't understand."

"I mean the house will be yours—no more rent payments."

Dewayne said, "How much will that come to?"

"$11,520." Tim was guessing that this would be about what the house would appraise for in its present condition.

"Tim, that don't make you a very good businessman. Why're you doin' this?"

"I have Someone who wants me to do it."

"Well, we don't know who that someone is, but you be sure and thank him or her for us!"

"I'm planning on doing that."

The fellows walked Tim back to his car. He said he would see them tomorrow and got into his car, but didn't drive off. He waited and watched the men walk back toward the hotel. They stopped and high-fived each other three times on the way back. Tim pulled out into the traffic, and again the smiling old man drove his Mercedes down the street.

He drove into the garage and started to walk into the house when he noticed Wally had two garbage cans ready to be put out on the front driveway for pick-up. He carried one can out and was surprised at how heavy it was. He carried out the second can which was much lighter. He turned to go back to the house when a searing hot pain hit him in the middle of his chest knocking him to one knee! He again got that very heavy feeling in his chest and arms like that day at SIMI! He was having a hard time breathing! He stayed in this position for some time until his breathing became easier, and the pain started to subside. He made his way into the garage and sat on a lawn chair. He stayed in the chair all of five minutes before going into the house.

He greeted Wally by saying, "I put the garbage out."

"I was wondering what was keeping you. I heard you drive in earlier. Busy morning?"

"Yes."

"What would you like for lunch?"

"I think I'll skip lunch—had a big breakfast."

"You OK, Sir?"

"Yes, just tired."

Tim took his shoes off and laid on his bed, mentally scolding himself. "I should have known better than to eat that big, greasy breakfast! The old stomach isn't what it used to be."

Wednesday morning Tim walked into Martin's office. "Good Morning, Mr. Mills."

"Mr. Mills…? Did I do something wrong?"

"No, just using the name I saw in the paper."

"Oh, you mean that Ark thing. Yeah we got it back. It's all locked up in bin number six."

"I can't believe it's back, Martin. It's like a dream where you move something, but it ends up back where you moved it from. Any coffee?"

"Help yourself. Know what you mean. I'm afraid I'm getting to feel like you did. The Ark's getting to me too! I don't think I had any choice but to help Israel out. SIMI can't afford not to ally Israel or the US!"

"You're in the driver's seat, Martin, and I hate back seat drivers. How long is it going to be here?"

"Don't know. They have some US troops guarding it. The army is being reimbursed for the security by anonymous donors here in the States."

"Unreal!"

"That's the best description I've heard to fit the situation. What're you up to today?"

"Oh, I came in to see if Snyder will loan me the white 'Jimmy' for the day?"

"What are you going to use the Jimmy for? You going to take some of your money to the bank?"

"No, I just have some things I have to haul. Need anything, give me a call, Martin."

"Thanks, Tim."

"Good morning, Pete."

"Good morning, Mr. Sorsen."

"Any chance I could use the white Jimmy today?"

"Sure. It's just sittin' there. Might have to jump it. It hasn't been started for a week or so."

"Be sure to fill out a rental agreement. This is for my personal use."

"OK, Sir. The key is over the visor."

Tim got into the van and it started right off. He drove to the Lincoln Hotel but got no answer to his knock on 417's door. He drove to Meeker Street and found a dirty bathtub, kitchen sink, toilet, and bathroom sink piled in the front yard of 1201.

Tim went into the house and found all four of the men working.

"Hi, Tim," Tommy said. "This is Frank."

"Good morning, Frank. Nice to meet you."

Frank didn't answer but wiped his hand on his pants and extended it to Tim for a nice firm handshake.

Dewayne came into the living room. "Morning, Tim."

"Good morning, Dewayne," Tim said, looking around the living room at tool boxes, canister vacuum cleaner, and a stepladder. "Where did you get all this stuff?"

"We borrowed 'em from friends and people we know."

Tim pointed toward the van out in front and told them how he had borrowed it to haul things. The men were elated for they had no way of hauling. They made arrangements to take the old fixtures to the dump, pick up the fixtures that they had stashed under the bridge on 14th Street, and pick up window glass at the lumber yard. They already had all the window measurements. Tim would pay for the glass and add it to the purchase price of the house.

The five men spent a fruitful day, each doing his task as if he had done it many times before. Tim did notice that if he overdid or tried lifting anything heavy, he would feel uncomfortable and become short of breath.

Tommy, who had been watching him, went over and talked to Dewayne. He patted Tim on the shoulder and said, "Why don't you take it easy. Let us do the heavy stuff, and you kind of get the other things. This ain't your kind of work nohow."

"I'll watch it. I really haven't felt too super the last couple of days."

Driving home after he left the men still working in their house, Tim mused about his day. That was the first time in his life that he had ever been to a city dump–not a pleasant place. Tommy explained that people put things that might be reusable way up on the edge of the dump. The unbelievably large combination bulldozers and compactors intentionally ignore them until toward the end of the day; then they doze it into the mass.

They spent no time looking for anything and merely unloaded their plumbing fixtures. Then they went to the bridge to pick up the other fixtures.

Tim continued driving home deep in thought. He drove by a house that had a kitchen stove, table with four chairs stacked on top, and two garbage cans out for garbage pick up. "Somebody else is doing some remodeling," he thought.

He drove on still thinking how resourceful Dewayne and his friends were–finding usable sinks, toilet, and finding the tools to work with. . . . "**Kitchen stove, table and chairs!** Where did I just see them?" He pulled over to the curb and remembered that he just passed them. "It can't be more than five or six blocks back on this street."

He turned the van around using somebody's driveway. He parked in front of the house with the prize garbage, knocked at the door, and a man about his age answered.

"Can I help you?"

"Yes, please. Are you throwing away the stove, table, and chairs by the driveway?"

"We sure are. Just finished remodeling the kitchen."

"Does the stove work?"

"Yeah, it's a good old stove. One chair has a busted rung. You want them?"

"I sure could use them."

"They're yours. Haul them away."

"I'll have to get some help. I can't lift, but I'll be right back. If you hear us out here, don't worry. Thank you very much."

"You're welcome."

Tim was returning to the van when the man yelled, "Hey, fellow, wait a minute. My boys are here helping me. We'll load that stuff for you." He disappeared into the house and didn't return for two or three minutes. Finally he came out with his sons. The one scanned the truck and the load and said, "It won't fit in the truck, Dad."

"Yes it will, Clarence. We can take the legs off of the table."

It was a tight fit, but they got it all in the van and got the doors closed. It was dark now, but Tim was able to see a pleasant looking woman holding a brown sack standing beside the man. She said, "This is some things that go with the table." He reached out and took the sack. "Thank you very much," he said and shook everyone's hand.

The van eased its way into the Mercedes' spot in the garage, as it was at SIMI. As he was walking around the van something very bright and colorful caught his eye in the van. It was sticking out of the brown sack. It looked like a loaf of bread! He opened the van door and took the sack and carried it into his kitchen.

It was a loaf of bread! It felt fresh. He also found a package of rice, two apples, one pound of ground beef, two cans of soup, a cello pack of cheese, and a pack of bologna.

Tim spread it out on the table and sat looking at it with tears running down his face. Wally came into the kitchen and was startled by his tearful face!

"Mr. Sorsen! Are you all right?"

Tim turned his very contrasting face toward Wally, a face with tears running down into a very happy smile. "I couldn't be or feel better, Wally! Sit down and let me tell you about my great day with its wonderful climax!"

Seeing Tim in his jeans on Friday, Betty said, "You look like you came to work today. After the prayer, she sent him over to serve coffee, tea, and water with a lady named Dora.

"Hi, Dora. I'm Tim."

"Hi, Tim. You new here?"

"Been here just once before."

"Ever serve coffee or tea before?"

"No."

"The secret's in the sugar. We keep it here. There's none on the table. They love sugar. Give them as much as they want, but keep the sugar dispenser here with us. Pour in some and ask, 'Is that enough?' Watch me."

"Will do."

"Giving out coffee and tea was much easier than dishing out soup. It was a lot more fun because it gave Tim a chance to visit more with the people, specially when there were two serving.

Betty came over with a man in tow. "Look who we have here," she said, tears in her eyes. The man was smiling so hard, his eyes were wrinkled shut. He had very beautiful teeth. It was Sam!

He stared at Sam, and he wiped his eyes as if to see better, but both his hand and his eyes became moist. He handed the glass of water he was holding to Dora. Tim, who was no hugger, put his arms around Betty and Sam. The three stood there with their arms around each other rejoicing. Betty said, "You guys never told me about this. What a surprise!"

A man in line said, "How about some coffee?"

Betty shot back, "You'll get your coffee in a minute, Orville!"

"OK, Betty."

"I better get Sam fed; you can talk to him later, Tim."

It was an average day at the kitchen. There were people frowning, people with straight faces, and people smiling. The greatest heartfelt smile was Sam's. Tim's and Betty's smiles were also heartfelt as they watched Sam smiling at those around him so much he didn't have time to eat.

Chapter 13

"But, as for me, I almost lost my balance; my feet all but slipped" (*Psalm* 73:2).

"It has been only a little over six weeks since the men had started fixing up the house on Meeker Street," thought Tim as he read the article in the Sunday paper: **"Homeless men beautify shack into a doll house."**

The article was accompanied by color photos of the "Shack" and the "Doll House." The three-bedroom frame house was now adorned with a coat of white paint, blue shutters, blue trim, a beautiful lawn, and shrubs.

The story told of the men's resourcefulness, how they obtained all the repairs, fixtures, and even furniture as discards. It told of how they got sod for the yard from people who were putting in driveways or rocking their yards. The shrubs also came from the city dump as discards.

Although the article was a beautiful, heartwarming story, Tim knew he was in trouble. The article went on to criticize the owners of the other homes on Meeker Street, saying how unbelievable it was that people were living in such filth and squaller! Councilwoman Lorna Williams promised an investigation into possible public health violations.

As he put the paper down, the phone rang right on cue!

Wally said, "It's a Mr. Auburn for you."

"Good morning, Bill."

"I don't know how damn good it is! Did you see today's paper?"

"I'm afraid I did, Bill."

"This could be real bad news for the Auburn Company, Tim. We're not an international company like SIMI. We depend on our good name here in the city and surrounding communities. People do business with us because we're a fine company, not a company which takes advantage of the poor!"

"I know, and I'm sorry it turned out this way."

"Oh, I'm not blaming you, Tim. I thought maybe you might have some idea how I might handle this situation. You've had some bad hands recently and made them look like a Royal Flush."

"Have you thought about using the situation to make your company look even better?"

"How would I do that?"

"Sell that property—house by house—to the homeless, at a price within their reach. You won't make any money. In fact you'll lose money, but you couldn't buy better PR anywhere for the same amount!" (". . . here or in Heaven," Tim thought.)

"But these people don't have any money!"

"Oh, lots of them are not completely destitute. Some have limited incomes, but not enough to buy or rent on today's market. They don't even try because they've lost all hope. They need somebody like the great Auburn Company to show them how."

"First somebody has to show the great Auburn Company how!"

"I know four men who might be able to handle that job."

"You mean the men who fixed up the one in the paper? Do you think that they might tackle something this big?"

"Bill, why don't I make arrangements for you to come to 1201 Meeker. See the house. Everything they've done has been inspected and approved by the city. Come meet the men and talk about your plans. Bill, if this thing hits the paper—and you know it will—you'll have more usable, discarded fixtures, appliances, furniture, building materials, and volunteer labor than you can handle!"

"Will you take me over there?"

"Be glad to."

"I don't know where you get these ideas, Sorsen. You must get them out of the sky or somewhere?"

"Amen."

"What?"

"Oh, nothing. Why don't I give you a call tomorrow and set up a meeting so you can see the house and meet the men?"

"Please do. And thanks, Tim!"

The next eight weeks were the most fulfilling and productive weeks in Tim's life. The "Auburn Project" was a huge success! The people of the community responded as he had predicted. Dewayne, Tommy, Blair, and Frank were busy working and directing the project. A national news magazine spent three days interviewing people working on the project, the people of the community, and photographing the activities and the homes. A major television network was planning a visit next week to cover the story. The Associated Press reported that projects like this have been started in six other cities across the country. Another city was renovating a hotel with discards. The hotel would then be used as temporary housing for the homeless.

Tim's activities were many and varied. He was known, for one, as the "Go For" in his white van, which he now rented from SIMI by the month. He also used the van to pick up donated food items for the Soup Kitchen.

The den had one lamp lit. Wally sat motionless looking out a window in a chair he had scooted up to the window. The Saturday afternoon news was on the TV behind him.

"Today's top story is again about the Ark of the Covenant, which was started in this city eleven months ago. We all know the story of the Ark and its adventurous stay here in this city and in the United States.

"Let us add another chapter to that story. We know that the Ark's scheduled tour was canceled due to the unusual number of heart attacks associated with the vast crowds that came to view the Ark.

"The Ark was then returned to Sorsen's International Machine Company, where it was first discovered. There it was to be prepared for shipment and to allow time for security precautions.

"It has now been disclosed by Mr. Martin Mills, Executive Vice President of SIMI, that two weeks ago, Israel made arrangements to bring the Ark back to Israel. SIMI advised this country that they as yet had not readied the vessel for shipment. They were told that such preparation was not necessary; it could be shipped in its present shipping container.

"The container was lifted by a forklift truck and was

proceeding to an awaiting truck when the forklift's front wheel struck a building support knocking its cargo to the floor smashing the crate, particularly one of its corners. The corner ended up a large hole, allowing a full view of the interior of the crate. There was no Ark in the container—only cement blocks!

"Mills said that the news was withheld so that his company could get Israel's response. The response was that no claim had ever been made that the Ark was in the container. The bill of lading read, 'The Ark of the Covenant Shipping Container.'

"True, the Israeli government realized that the rest of the world assumed that the Ark was in the container. This government took advantage of this assumption and returned a container with the Ark in it. Where was it returned to? Israel's official reply is that it has been returned to where it came from and will always remain.

"For further coverage on the Ark, stay tuned immediately after this newscast for an NBC special on the Ark of the Covenant.

"We must add some sad news to this story, which will be of particular interest to the local viewing audience. Tim Sorsen died this morning. His body was discovered at 7:30 a.m. by his house attendant of many years. You'll remember Tim Sorsen as President of SIMI where the Ark first made its appearance. Cause of death is unknown. It appeared to be heart failure; however, there will be an autopsy to determine cause. It seems Sorsen was holding in his hands an open match box that had been sealed with cellophane tape. A pen knife which was probably used to open the box was found nearby. Along with the autopsy, the box will be tested for drug traces.

"More news after these announcements."

> *"I owed peace offerings, and today I have*
> *fulfilled my vows;*
> *"So I came out to meet you, to look for you,*
> *and I have found you!"*
> (*Proverbs* 7:14-15).

About the Author

Frank Callison has a BA degree in Business Administration and was formerly a salesman, sales manager, and general manager. He is a fledgling biblical scholar who has spent many years studying the Bible, most recently completing a four-year accredited Bible study course at the Catholic Biblical School, Archdiocese of Denver.

Mr. Callison considers himself a good listener and recorder. As a salesman and public speaker, he knew what his audience wanted to hear and how to impress them with his product and the company he represented. He spent many hours writing sales letters, newsletters, advertising, inspirational letters, and speeches. He attributes a great deal of his success to this writing ability.

Combined with his first world experiences, Mr. Callison has balanced his insights by serving in soup lines, raising funds for and communing with the very poor and homeless for over a decade. He is 69 years old, is married and has five children and six grandchildren.

THE RIEHLE FOUNDATION . . .

The Riehle Foundation is a non-profit, tax-exempt, charitable organization that exists to produce and/or distribute Catholic material to anyone, anywhere.

The Foundation is dedicated to the Mother of God and her role in the salvation of mankind. We believe that this role has not diminished in our time, but on the contrary has become all the more apparent in this the era of Mary as recognized by Pope John Paul II, whom we strongly support.

During the past five years the foundation has distributed over four million books, films, rosaries, bibles, etc. to individuals, parishes, and organizations all over the world. Additionally, the Foundation sends materials to missions and parishes in a dozen foreign countries.

Donations forwarded to The Riehle Foundation for the materials distributed provide our sole support. We appreciate your assistance, and request your prayers.

IN THE SERVICE OF JESUS AND MARY
All for the honor and glory of God!

The Riehle Foundation
P.O. Box 7
Milford, OH 45150
U.S.A.

Faith Publishing Company has been organized as a service for the publishing and distribution of materials that reflect Christian values, and in particular, the teachings of the Catholic Church.

It is dedicated to publication of only those materials that reflect such values.

Faith Publishing Company also publishes books for The Riehle Foundation. The Foundation is a non-profit, tax-exempt producer and distributor of Catholic books and materials worldwide and also supplies hospital and prison ministries, churches, and mission organizations.

For more information on the publications of Faith Publishing Company, contact:

P.O. BOX 237
MILFORD, OHIO 45150

ADDITIONAL TITLES AVAILABLE
Contact The Riehle Foundation

A Heavenly Journey
by Veralyn R. Alpha

This fictional journey of a young minister transported back to the early Church is a clever defense of the Catholic Faith. It skillfully combines biblical and historical facts.

96 pages   ISBN: 1-880033-15-1 $4.50

Six Short Stories on the
Via Dolorosa
by Ernesto V. Laguette

Fictional stories of what the Scourger, Simon of Cyrene, Veronica, Gamaliel, Longinus, and Dismas might have experienced during our Lord's Passion. Includes new, very moving Stations of the Cross meditations.

144 pages   ISBN: 1-877678-29-5 $4.00

Prayer of the Warrior
by Michael H. Brown

A fascinating investigative report of the rising tide of occultism and demonism — and Heaven's response. Many readers have written to say they were profoundly affected by this book. Blows the lid off evil, and shows that God's intervention is always at hand.

256 pages   ISBN: 1-880033-10-0 $11.00